Adolphe Danziger

In the Confessional and The following

Adolphe Danziger

In the Confessional and The following

ISBN/EAN: 9783741181542

Manufactured in Europe, USA, Canada, Australia, Japa

Cover: Foto ©Andreas Hilbeck / pixelio.de

Manufactured and distributed by brebook publishing software (www.brebook.com)

Adolphe Danziger

In the Confessional and The following

I dedicate this volume of unpretentious stories to the 𝔏𝔦𝔱𝔢𝔯𝔞𝔯𝔶 𝔖𝔱𝔯𝔲𝔤𝔤𝔩𝔢𝔯𝔰 *of the Pacific Coast, and to*

MARCUS B. LEVY, ESQ.,

In Law my Father,
In Fact my Friend;

By whose many favors I was enabled to pursue my literary labors, of which this is the smallest part.

G. A. D.

In the Confessional.

IN THE CONFESSIONAL.

I.

THE Church of Our Lady of the Sacred Heart in Paris was filled with worshipers, kneeling, and devoutly counting their rosaries. A number of the fairest women in the parish knelt by the door, near the priest's confessional, waiting their turn to confess to the handsome priest, who had lately arrived — it was said — from Rome. In the green-curtained inclosure sat the priest, his head bent toward the narrow opening, speaking solace and encouragement to all those who sought forgiveness for transgressions.

He was a remarkably handsome man, — Father Felician. His face — clean shaven

— was plump and rosy; his neck and hands were of alabaster whiteness; the latter were almost effeminate in their shape and elegance. In his eyes was reflected Heaven's own mildness, and his mouth would have expressed divine innocence and gentleness, were it not for a sharp cut about the corners, which marred the perfect harmony of that angelic face. In spite of Father Felician's five and fifty years, there was not a white streak in the glossy blackness of his hair.

His voice, usually resonant and manly, became low and tender as he greeted the penitents with a soft *Pax vobiscum;* it thrilled the souls of the fair sinners and made them more fervent and devout. He listened to the narration of trivial shortcomings with priestly grace and fatherly kindness.

It is needless to state that Father Felician had not an enemy in the world. Was he not the anointed of the Lord? His consoling words were like the balm of Gilead upon an open wound, and his sage advice as tender and benign as that of an elder brother. Men and women alike loved and admired him. "He was born to be a priest of God," they would say. This popular sentiment was shared by his Bishop, who never missed an opportunity to affirm the excellent qualities of Father Felician.

Holy Mother Church seemed proud of so handsome, so eloquent, and so beloved a son, for she, too, showered upon him exceptional favors.

And no wonder. His sermons were so stirring, so strong, so persuasive and logical, that the church register was full of the names of his converts from the ranks of Protestants. His sermon on the Christmas morning on which the sad event to be told in this story took place was a masterpiece of rhetorical dexterity, logical acumen, and Christian piety; it was a glorious exposition of the Saviour's love, of joy in Heaven and peace and happiness among men. And now the fair parishioners thronged around his confessional, watching eagerly the green curtains to see those who had received absolution leave with bright and smiling faces.

Among those waiting their turn to pour out their sorrow-laden hearts before the Throne of Mercy was a woman dressed in black and closely veiled; she was evidently a stranger, for she knelt alone, and no one seemed to know her.

She had waited for some time, and at length grew quite restless. She rose and gently made her way toward the confessional, and addressed the woman whose turn it was next to enter the sacred inclosure: "May I ask you to let me enter first, dear madame? I am very unfortunate, and I have no time to wait."

Her tone was so sad and her foreign accent so charming, her figure so imposing and her dress so somber, that the amiable Parisienne involuntarily moved aside and deferentially asked the stranger to precede her. The stranger expressed her thanks, and knelt. When her turn came she took a vial from her pocket, and, putting it to her lips, deliberately drank its contents.

The woman, who noticed this, marveled, as it was not customary for any one to taste anything before confession; but she thought no more of it until an hour later, when she recalled it with a shudder.

"Blessed be the name of our Lord Jesus Christ," said Father Felician, softly, as the woman in black knelt before the opening in the confessional. But as she made no response, he continued: "In all eternity. Amen."

"Who are you, my daughter?" he continued, placing his ear close to the opening.

"I am an unfortunate woman, driven to despair, crime, and death by the cruelty of a merciless man," said the woman, hardly above a whisper.

Father Felician sighed, as if he felt the burden of sorrow that bore down this poor, forlorn creature before him.

"Forgive, my daughter. Whoso forgiveth shall be forgiven by our Father who is in heaven." Father Felician spoke those words solemnly, softly, sweetly, and full of divine compassion.

" Ah, Father, there are sins which cannot be forgiven, — not if one is impenitent."

There was a wild look in the woman's eyes as she said that. Father Felician did not seem to have noticed it, for he said: "But you are penitent, my daughter."

A tired look came into her face, and she leaned her head against the railing.

"I am dying, Father," she said; "and before I die, I desire to confess — and — ah — yes — to be forgiven, — if there can be forgiveness for such as I."

Her voice grew faint, a pallor spread over her face, and a shudder ran through her frame.

Father Felician knew that a poor, sinful creature knelt before him, who needed the comforting words of a father and the divine solace of God's anointed. His heart went out toward this young and beautiful sinner, for this was undeniably true; the face before him was of the most exquisite beauty. Creatures like those are always beset by the flesh and the devil, and the designers of evil never rest until they get them into their power. She is innocent, — she is certainly innocent, — thought Father Felician. And now his words came with æolian softness.

"Have courage, my daughter," he said. "Man is sinful, but true repentance leads to grace. As is written: 'If thy sins be as scarlet, they shall be made as white as snow.' In the name of Him who saved the world, I bid you have courage."

These words seemed to overpower the poor woman. She seemed broken-hearted; her head sank on her breast, and sigh after sigh escaped her lips.

"Father," she cried, "I am dying, not with disease, but by my own hand. I have taken poison." Father Felician started back, shocked.

"Daughter, what have you done? I will get you help."

"Useless, Father. There is no antidote

to the poison I have taken; it is as sure as fate, and as cruel. Call no one, Father, but listen, although I am afraid the task of telling my sad story may prove too difficult for me."

"This is terrible, my daughter; let me call a physician; there may be help for you, and you may yet live to be happy," said the priest.

"I am past help and past happiness, Father. In less than two hours I shall be dead; and if you will not hear me I shall die without confessing," said the lady, resolutely.

Now, Father Felician would let no penitent Christian die without absolution if he could help it. Young, beautiful, and dying, — ah, how really sad and disagreeable the latter fact was!

"Proceed, then, my daughter," said the priest, sadly; "and may God strengthen you."

"Before I tell you my sad story, I beg you, Father, to accept this; it contains my my last will and testament. You may read it now." With this she handed the priest a small envelope. The will must have been remarkably brief, the envelope was so small. So, indeed, thought Father Felician, as he somewhat thoughtfully gazed upon the diminutive letter cover in his hand, upon which was written his name, in a bold, masculine hand.

A student of physiognomy would have observed the change in the priest's face after he had read the will. His color came and went like lightning.

The will was certainly quite brief. It read as follows: "The sum of 900,000 francs, which I give and bequeath to Father Felician of the Church of Our Lady of the Sacred Heart, is to revert to the Church after his death."

This peculiar document was duly signed by the testatrix and two witnesses. Father Felician was quite surprised. He had never before seen the lady, nor had he ever heard her name mentioned. The latter —Da Poniatowska— was a Polish name, and he knew no one by that name.

The lady, however, gave him no time for reflection.

"I have no explanation for my action," she said. "I am alone, and you may as well have the use of that money as the state. But now, I entreat you, Father, hear me; hear the story of my life, and judge of the magnitude of my sins."

"God's mercy is without end," said the priest. "Jesus forgave the murderer on the cross. Tell me your story."

II.

About ten Russian miles from the city of Warsaw, on an eminence overlooking the valley of the Vistula, stood the ancient castle of the widowed Count Potosky. The Count and his only child, the Countess Wanda, occupied the castle six months of each year; the other six months they spent in Paris or in St. Petersburg. The Countess Wanda was universally acknowledged to be the most beautiful woman in the empire. At her feet princes had knelt, hungry for a look from her glorious eyes. Men had fought duels and had gone mad on her account, but no one could ever boast that Wanda, by word or look, had ever encouraged their advances. She was not a coquette,. and would not deign to play with men's hearts; the people that courted her found no favor in her eyes, and she did not try to like them. The Count was not at all satisfied.

"You are too fastidious," he would say.

She then kissed his forehead, and asked him whether he would like to get rid of her.

"No," said the Count; "but you will have to marry some time; I shall not live forever, and you need a protector."

"Whenever I shall see the man I like," she replied, "I will tell you, and you may invite him. Until then — wait."

The Count did not wait very long, for very soon Countess Wanda met Count Vladislav de Turnisky, whom she loved with a devotion born of a tender heart and spotless soul. But she also met Vladislav's friend, Jan Felix Kanigefsky, and her sad fate.

Kanigefsky loved her with a most unholy passion, and seeing his friend succeed where he had failed, his vindictive nature turned against the friend of his youth, and he hated them both with the bitterest, most unrelenting hatred.

He swore their ruin, and he never rested until he had accomplished his revenge.

Wanda paid dearly for the blissful moments of a short love; the agony of her soul overshadowed the sunshine of her wedded life. Kanigefsky was more cruel than Satan, his rage hotter than hell, and his vindictiveness as deep as the bottomless pit.

III.

The city of Warsaw and its famous citadel at Praga were alive with soldiers of all grades and descriptions. The country swarmed with imperial troops, who were quartered in the houses of free farmers and the castles of the nobles.

The massing of troops in the Vistula district was due to the maneuvers which were to be held in the vicinity of the city of Warsaw.

The nobles entertained the officers of the army with balls and parties. The castle of Count Vladislav de Turnisky was the rendezvous of the highest grades. The beautiful Countess was the main attraction. On the third day after the maneuvers were opened the Count and Countess, with their ten-year-old daughter, witnessed the grand spectacle at the special invitation of the commander.

A sham battle was planned. The field of action was a plain, where a large body of soldiers were stationed, while the attacking forces came from the imperial forest to the right, where the Count and his family had taken their positions and were watching with eager interest.

The roar of cannon was deafening, and the smoke suffocating, but the curious spectators did not mind it much; the novelty excited and fascinated them. Suddenly the Count uttered a cry and fell. The Countess, who had leaned on his arm, seeing her husband fall, believed that he had fainted, and called for help. The General, on hearing what happened, dispatched his physician. The latter looked at the Count and shook his head. Bending down, he then placed his hand upon the Count's heart, and, rising, calmly said, "He is beyond help."

"What do you mean?" cried the Countess.

"I am extremely grieved to tell your ladyship that the Count is dead."

"Dead!" cried the Countess, and fell upon the body in a swoon. She was carried to her carriage, and was attended by the physician whose words had dealt her such a hard blow. As soon as she had recovered, the doctor left her, and ordered some men to carry the Count to a carriage. But as they lifted the body, the physician gave a low whistle, for beneath it was found a pool of blood.

When Valera, the Count's little daughter, saw the blood on the ground she screamed and became hysterical.

"Papa is cut," she cried. "Papa is cut."

This drew the attention of the Countess to the body of her husband. But she was strangely composed as she asked the physician where the blood came from. "It must have been a stray shot that killed him," said the surgeon.

Count Vladislav de Turnisky lay in state for three days. Officers of all grades visited the castle to view the remains of one who in life had been most conspicuous for hospitality. Some there were who went to see the beautiful Countess, but all were respectful; this somewhat ameliorated the sorrow of the stricken widow.

The night before the burial she refused to let any one but herself watch by the loved one. Valera begged to stay; she was gently but firmly commanded to go to bed. Poor child! she could not sleep, while her beautiful mother was weeping by the side of her dead father. She put her ear to the keyhole and listened.

Suddenly she heard the hall door open, and by the heavy tread concluded that a man had entered the room.

The child thought she heard her mother give a suppressed scream, but she was afraid to enter the saloon, because her mother had told her to go to bed. All at once Valera heard her mother say: "What do you want, sir?"

IN THE CONFESSIONAL. 23

"I want you, Countess Wanda," said a masculine voice.

"Begone, sir," cried the Countess, "or I shall call the servants."

"You will do nothing of the kind," the man said.

Then the child heard her mother utter a muffled scream, and all was quiet. Valera was too frightened to move. She slipped into her little bed, drew the cover over her face, and soon fell asleep. There was great consternation in the castle the next morning when it was found that the Countess had disappeared.

They hunted high and low, but they could not find her; she was gone. The Count was buried, and Valera went to live with her aunt in the city of Warsaw.

IV.

Eight years had gone by. Valera had grown to be a young lady of great beauty; but all through the years she never for a moment forgot her mother, and when she went to school she frequently stopped and looked after ladies, in hopes of finding her. One day, as Valera was on her way home from church, she was accosted by a woman, who placed her hand on Valera's arm. The latter turned and uttered a scream; the woman's face was frightfully mutilated. In spite of the distressing sight, Valera mastered herself, and asked the woman what she wanted, at the same time handing her her purse.

The woman did not seem to see it; she gazed steadily into the girl's eyes and asked her whether her name was Valera de Turnisky. The girl answered, and again asked what she could do for her.

The woman's mutilated face grew pale as she murmured: "It is true,—she does not know me. No one will ever know me again."

Two big tears rolled down her slashed and scarred cheeks. Valera stood and looked at the woman, but her gaze seemed to wander beyond the woman into the distance. Suddenly she began to shiver, and pressed her hands against her heart. She knew not how it happened,—she uttered the word "Mother." At this the woman uttered a cry and fell down in a faint. Being brought to by passers-by, the first words she uttered were, "Thank God, she knows me!"

Yes. Valera's instinct was true; the woman with the scarred and mutilated face was none other than the once beautiful Countess Wanda.

Valera wanted to bring her mother to her

aunt's residence, but the poor Countess implored her not to shock the people; she preferred, she said, to go away and live in seclusion the short time she still had to live. Valera put a heavy veil about her mother's face and brought her to a hotel, after which she hastened home and told her aunt that she was going to leave at once for the country. An hour later, Valera and her mother were on the road to her old home.

"It was in this room," said Valera's mother on the morning after her arrival, "that I sat and watched by the side of your father's dead body, when the door suddenly opened and Kanigefsky stood before me. He was dressed in the uniform of a colonel, and had on a great-coat. I was so shocked at his sudden appearance that I did not know what to say; because he had been your father's bitterest enemy ever since I refused to marry him. Still, I thought that your father's death had softened his heart, and that he had come to offer his condolence. I would not believe otherwise, although I could see that his eyes were aglow with hatred.

"I asked him to be seated, but he refused, at the same time uttering an imprecation against your poor father. I was shocked, and asked him what he wanted. He told me that he wanted me. The passion in his eyes frightened me. I told him to go. I was at the same time moving toward the bell-cord to call the servants. But he evidently knew of my intention; for as quick as a flash he was by my side, and, throwing his great-coat over me, took me and carried me out of the room. I was placed in a carriage; my abductor took his seat by my side, and we were driven away.

"Shortly after, Kanigefsky took the coat off me; and seeing that I was completely in his power, I begged him to be merciful. But he only laughed.

"'You shall amuse me first,' he said, with a coarse laugh.

"'For heaven's sake, what do you want of me?' I cried, horrified.

"'You refused to be my wife; you shall now be my slave, and beware how you act. I shall enforce obedience through my orderly.'

"My heart stood still at the thought of the horrible fate that awaited me, but I swore to die rather than yield to him. Oh, what shall I tell you of the many sorry days and anxious nights I spent in the house of that monster? I was always on the watch, and frustrated his schemes. At last, maddened by drink, he came into my room and caught me in his arms. But, like a flash, I buried my penknife in his breast. His rage became uncontrollable. He took his sword and deliberately slashed and hacked my face. I fell on my knees and begged for mercy, but this infuriated him still more. He kicked me with the heel of his boot, and in his madness would have killed me had not his servant entered and prevented him. He at once turned upon the servant, but the latter was too quick. He knew the brute, and was prepared. He jumped behind a large marble table, and covered his master with a revolver. This had the desired effect. 'I will not stay with you any longer,' said the servant. 'You are a maniac and a murderer. First you shot down the Count, then you brutalized his wife. You ought to be put in an insane asylum.'

"Poor fellow, he paid dearly for his bravery. The monster permitted him to leave the room, but had him arrested a few minutes later and flogged to death. Months afterward, when I had barely recovered from that horrible treatment, I found myself in convict's clothes, on the way to Siberia.

"'Your own father would not recognize you now,' were the words he called after me when I was marched off.

"One year ago I had been given permission to return home. I thanked God for the privilege; for I hoped to see you, my child. But the fear that you would not recognize me, and that you might turn away in horror from your poor mother, has nearly robbed me of my senses. My daughter," the Countess continued, emphasizing each word, "I shall die soon. Promise me to avenge your father's death and your mother's sufferings upon that wretch. Hunt him down if you have to go to every land under the sun."

V.

In the confessional sat Father Felician, listening to that narrative of passion and crime. He was deadly pale, and big beads of perspiration stood upon his forehead.

"You are innocent, my daughter," said the priest. "You have magnified your sins."

"Oh no, Father! I have not," said the woman. "I have had murder in my heart for a number of years, and have been, I think, greatly sinful; for I am the daughter of that unfortunate woman, Countess Wanda, and I have kept my promise most faithfully."

"Did you slay the Colonel Kanigefsky?" the priest asked.

"No," replied the lady. "Soon after my mother's death, which occurred a few weeks after her return from Siberia, I sold our estates, and as my aunt, too, had died and had left me all her property, I sold all and moved to Paris. Before I left, however, I tried to find the Colonel, but was told that he had left the army many years ago, and no one seemed to know whither he had gone. I searched for him in every country in Europe, but in vain.

"Last week I returned to Paris from Rome, where I had lived for several months. As I have attended your church for some time, I concluded to bequeath my fortune to you, and in case of your death, to the Church.

"My agent in Rome, who knew my mother, and through me learned of her sad fate, begged me to desist from the useless search.

"'Kanigefsky is dead,' my agent said. 'If he were alive, we would have discovered his whereabouts ere this. But, my dear young lady, you need rest. Go to Paris, and keep quiet. I shall have my eyes open and write you from time to time.'

"This morning I received a dispatch from my agent, informing me that Kanigefsky was in Paris. But I was tired of life, and before going to confession I took poison that is sure to kill me now."

"Does the dispatch state where Kanigefsky is?" asked the priest.

"Yes, Father; do you care to see it?" the woman inquired.

"Let me see it, my daughter," said the priest, in a trembling voice

"Here," she said.

Quick as thought she arose, thrust her hand through the opening of the confessional, and pushed in with all her force; then she staggered backward, and fell in a heap upon the ground. Simultaneously with this a cry was heard — a cry of agony. The people heard it, but did not understand its meaning; a moment later they were horror-stricken when they saw Father Felician draw the green curtains aside, blood rushing from his nose and mouth, a dagger with a jeweled handle up to the hilt in his breast.

He tried to speak, but could not, the blood in his throat causing a gurgling sound; a moment later he fell his entire length upon the floor. A scene of confusion ensued; women screamed and fainted, and men pushed their way to the confessional.

They found Father Felician dead, and, near by, the lady in black.

She was dead, too, and, clutched tightly, in her hand was found a dispatch from Rome, which read as follows:—

"Jan Felix Kanigefsky, the renegade and murderer of your parents, after leaving the army, entered the theological seminary in Rome, and took holy orders twelve years ago. He is now known as Father Felician, the priest of the Church of Our Lady of the Sacred Heart.

"RAUL."

THE FOLLOWING:

	PAGE
THE FATED STAR	37
A CHRISTMAS PROMISE	77
THE STORY OF VLADIMIR	94
THE AUTOMATIC EXECUTIONER	133
A SACRIFICE TO SCIENCE	154
THE FOREIGN ELEMENT	216
THE FATAL LETTER	239
A MIDNIGHT SONG	277

THE FATED STAR.

I.

"IF you want to succeed on the stage you must live by the 'rule of four'; it leads to fame and fortune," said Miss Ludmilla Lassen.

"The 'rule of four'! I never heard of such a rule. I know of the 'rule of three,' but of no other," replied Miss Antonette de Fallon.

"The 'rule of three' is a flat failure in this case. An actress who deviates from the rule of four lives in poverty and dies ingloriously. Having reached the pinnacle of fame, she may discard one or two, but to start without them is out of the question."

"Perhaps this is the reason why I do not succeed. I have no idea of your rule."

"Precisely. You are young, beautiful, and talented, and yet you are a mere cipher. You don't get a first-rate engagement; you are not popular."

"But what shall I do?"

"Do! Study the 'rule of four'; but be careful to study the proper rule; if you make a mistake, you are lost."

"But I am ignorant of the elementary principles of your rule? Can't you tell me the rudiments of the same?"

"Yes."

"What are they?"

"Men."

"Men! What would you want me do?"

"Don't be alarmed, Tony. I don't mean that you should throw yourself away on every flirt; for an actress without dignity, womanhood, and virtue cannot be a true actress. Our art demands dignity, but, withal, we need men — a certain class, at least — to assist us."

"Mamma has warned me against all assistance proffered by men."

"Bless your mamma! If it were not for your mamma, you would be far ahead in the profession."

"Don't say that, Ludi dear; my mamma is the best woman living."

"I don't deny that; but she cannot make you a success so long as you and she are prejudiced against men. An actress needs admirers. If you can't make up your mind to that, you had better leave the stage."

"I can't do that; I could not exist without its excitement."

"And you are willing to make your way on the stage?"

"Yes."

"And study the rudiments of the 'rule of four'?"

"Yes."

"Very well, you shall have your first lesson this evening at the dance, — for there is going to be a dance at the 'Casino,' and we will be there. But now let us take a walk to the Brunnen; a glass of mineral water will do us good."

II.

The remarkable conversation of the previous chapter, was held between two ladies at their temporary residence in a mountain village near one of the summer resorts in the Tyrol. Both were actresses in the Burg Theater, in the city of Vienna. Ludmilla Lassen was a brunette, tall, imperious, beautiful, and intelligent. She was famous and wealthy, and could well afford to advise her friend Antonette, who was much younger, and of whom she was very fond. Ludmilla was about thirty years of age, while her friend was one and twenty. The beauty of the latter was superlative, but she had been catalogued by the director of the Burg Theater as a "beautiful acquisition without talent." Actresses know what that means in a country where histrionic success is not achieved by a beautiful face, but by genius or commanding talent, both of which are more potent than birth, wealth, and influence. Antonette by no means lacked talent; but, somehow, she had never been given a part in which she might have excelled. Besides, the military and aristocratic civilians had tacitly ignored her as soon as it became known that her mother acted the Cerberus against their licentious advances. The press never mentioned

Antonette in her fifth-rate roles, and thus the poor girl suffered the mortification of being tolerated on the stage and neglected by the public until the famous Ludmilla noticed her. Her sententious expressions encouraged Antonette, and she concluded to live and work by Ludmilla's advice.

III.

"I say, Seebag," said Baron Zano, a Hungarian magnate of eccentric proclivities, "did you notice those two girls at the Brunnen this morning? Devilish fine girls! Wonder who they are?"

"Why, don't you know Ludmilla Lassen, Baron? Where are your eyes?" cried Seebag, a noted *litterateur* and playwright from Vienna.

"The devil you say! Is this Ludmilla? Ah, immense! But who is the other?"

"Don't know; some friend, I suppose. I didn't see her close enough; can't tell."

"Suppose we invite them to the dance to-night?" said Baron Zano.

"Capital idea," Seebag cried. "Ah! see, Baron! there comes the trinity, — Dr. Grau, Director Kraut, and Count Mehrau. Hello, gentlemen!" he cried, addressing the new-comers. "Fraulein Ludmilla Lassen is rusticating in the village. Baron Zano and myself have just conspired to invite them to the dance to-night. Let's go in a body, and do honor to the Muses."

"*C'est charmant*," said Count Mehrau, a fat little Prussian, with small, blinking eyes. "Great idea; let us go."

"Hi-hi-hi! so my Ludmilla has taken her quarters here," said Director Kraut. "'T is lucky, very lucky indeed," he continued, stroking his abdomen, which protruded like a good-sized beer-barrel. "Let us go, gentlemen; the gods are with us. Yes, indeed!"

Dr. Grau, the merciless critic, alone was silent. He did not show any excessive joy; it would have been beneath his dignity to manifest any undue enthusiasm for an actress, whom he might annihilate with his pen at any time. His companions seemed to know his sentiments and made no observation. It was a fact known in all circles of society that Dr. Grau was incorruptible; his feeling — if he had any — never befogged his judgment, and the beauty of an actress, if she lacked talent, made him so much more bitter against her. "A puppet of clay without expression, without a soul," he would say in his report. "Unworthy of notice; still, a menace to the general appreciation of talent by her unhallowed, unnecessary, and undeserved presence."

Poor Ludmilla! it took her years to win

a word of approval from Dr. Grau; and it was owing to this fact that he accompanied the rest to the village.

IV.

"What do you think of the blonde, Grau? Isn't she superb? Is a member of the Burg Theater, too. By the gods! never thought she was so beautiful. De Fallon comes of a good family. Mother is said to be a Satan. But isn't she great?" said the Director.

"It depends upon what you consider great, Kraut," replied Dr. Grau. "I have not discovered any greatness in her. A woman of her stamp always reminds me of the biblical sentence, that it is easier for a camel to pass through the eye of a needle than for rich men to enter heaven. In this case I should say that it was easier for a camel to pass through the eye of a needle than for Mlle. de Fallon to have talent, — to be, as you expressed it, great."

"The devil take you, pedants!" cried the Director, mopping his brow. "What do you think of her, Seebag?"

"That she is a dream, a poem, a love-song; that I have never seen her peer in beauty; that she is an inspiration."

"She may be all that," chimed in the eccentric Baron. "But I hate commonplace women. I worship an eccentric woman, — a woman that don't mope and pout and sigh and weep, and drown me in an ocean of brats. I want —"

"Ah, pap-er-la-pap!" broke in Count Mehrau; "that is nothing. My ideal is the divine Ludmilla, — Ludmilla the charming, the fiery, the great, the Rachel of Austria! Ah, Ludmilla, there is nothing like thee on earth! Come in, gentlemen, let's drink a bottle to Ludmilla the divine, and to that other star, who borrows her radiance from the only Sun in Vienna! *Allons, messieurs!*"

They drank deep and long, until the Baron forgot his eccentricities and praised Ludmilla, and Count Mehrau swore he loved Antonette; until the Director shed tears of regret at not having recognized her charms heretofore, and Dr. Grau acknowledged the supremacy of beauty over talent; and Bacchus, laurel-wreathed upon his hogshead, blinked and smiled approval.

V.

"So, Tony dear," said Ludmilla, "let us arrange a plan of action. The lesson in the 'rule of four' begins. You are very lucky. The ciphers have appeared unbidden; it will depend upon your mathematical skill to keep them intact; and rely upon my assistance in all matters."

"I will do my best, dearest; but I am quite at sea in this matter. I don't know how to begin," Antonette replied.

"Well, we will see. There is, to begin with, Herr Seebag, an author and playwright. You must catch him first. For, in order to succeed, you must have a lover who can write a good play, and this he must write for you especially; he must make you famous."

"You seem to think this quite an easy matter; besides, Herr Seebag—". Here Antonette blushed to the roots of her hair.

Ludmilla gave a long, shrill whistle.

"The fish is caught, eh? Never mind, Tony, it will come out all right. But at present you must act. You understand, you must act a part; have as much or as little sentimentality with Herr Seebag as you like, but don't forget the others. Herr Seebag is but one of the principles in the 'rule of four.' The second principle, or cipher, shall be Baron Zano."

"For what purpose?" asked Antonette.

"You goose! Don't you know that you need some one to care for and supply your wardrobe?"

"I don't dream of such a thing,' replied Antonette.

"My dear Tony, if you desire to make headway on the stage, it is absolutely necessary that you should have a second admirer, who shall regard it his greatest happiness to lay at your feet the best Parisian gowns, — or pay for them, which amounts to the same. This by no means obliges you to anything; the longer you lead him on, the better for you. Your moral principles are not in the least endangered by this."

"You must not forget, Ludi dear, that—"

"That you are the daughter of an aristocratic father, who was a colonel in the Austrian army," the vivacious Ludmilla interrupted her friend; "but who imprudently left his family nothing but a small monthly allowance. Well, now, I think we had better stop here. You are not made for the stage."

"Go on, dear," cried Antonette, "I'll do as you say; you know best."

"That's a dear girl," said Ludmilla, kissing her friend. "The Baron is crazy for eccentric women. I know that of old. If you can manage him,—and you must do it,—he is not only yours, but you have made a most important step in the right direction. The other two ciphers can be managed in the city. There they will prove of considerable service; but at present they are indifferent. Will you go ahead?"

"I will, dearest," cried Antonette. "You are so good, so unselfish."

"Not at all," said Ludmilla. "I am selfish; I want the satisfaction of knowing that your future success is my creation, and that I shall have some one to take my place — for I shall retire soon — who is worthy of the laurels. I love you, and you shall succeed me."

Antonette threw herself in her friend's arms and wept tears of joy and gratitude.

"Now, remember, Tony," said Ludmilla, "with Seebag you must play the part of the ideal maiden, innocent and full of feeling, — he is a poet, you know. The Baron, on the other hand, you must treat badly; the more brutally you treat him, the more he will worship you. You must tell him that you hate women; that your sole regret in life is not having been born a man. Then you may be a little whimsical, — just a little, you know. So, and now to work, young woman," Ludmilla concluded, with a laugh. "It is time to dress; and pray, remember, wear nothing but white, and some forget-me-nots on the left side of your *coiffure*."

VI.

It was a day or two after the dance. The weather was hot and sultry, and Antonette de Fallon, acting upon the advice of her friend Ludmilla, sought the cool shade of the woods. Before long, Seebag found her. She was occupied winding a wreath of oak-leaves. The blush which mantled her brow and crimsoned her cheeks was not in her "programme," nor was her maidenly bashfulness mere acting. The poet, delighted to renew the acquaintance under such bucolic circumstances, asked permission to take a seat by her side. This being granted, an animated conversation was fast assisting their respective endeavors. Antonette's lustrous eyes kindled an unquenchable fire in Seebag's poetic breast, and when Antonette naïvely placed the wreath upon the poet's brow, he became her slave, body and soul.

On their homeward walk, Seebag said to Antonette: "You have given me so much pleasure; you have been so gracious, Miss de Fallon, that I wish I knew how to repay your kindness. But poor as any attempt on my part may prove, I beg you will command me. I am at your disposal."

"Are you, indeed?" said Antonette, with downcast eyes.

"Certainly, gracious Fraulein. I await your commands."

"Then," cried Antonette, lifting her

eyes, in which shone the light of triumph, "then write me a part, Herr Seebag."

"You are too modest, Miss de Fallon."

"Not at all; a new play by you, in which I had to play the principal part, would be more valuable to me than jewels," the girl replied.

Flattered by her praise and fired by the luster in her eyes and the smile on her lips, Seebag said:

"Very well, you shall have the play."

"But you must give me a role peculiarly adapted for me alone. I want something entirely out of the common."

"Ah!" said Seebag, "I have a play the title of which is 'The Fated Star,' but the heroine is one of those capricious and eccentric creatures whom no man with a soul in his body can respect, and which is as different from you — thank God! — as black is from white."

"Ah, that would certainly be an excellent part for me!" Antonette remarked. "One always plays that character best which is entirely opposed to one's own nature, you know."

"This is quite indisputable," Seebag replied, "especially one with as much beauty, breeding, and talent as you. Your word is law; you shall have the play."

"Thank you, very much," Antonette said with a sweet smile; and having reached the cottage where she and Ludmilla resided she gave him her hand. "I thank you," she repeated. Seebag kissed her soft and slender hand and left.

VII.

Baron Zano, finding the people at the Casino too commonplace, rented a cabin high up in the mountains. His hostess just suited him, she swore like a trooper and smoked a pipe. A day or two after the sentimental meeting with the poet Seebag, Antonette, dressed in elegant hunter's costume, stepped into the Baron's cabin. She was accompanied by a hunter, who carried a buck she had just shot.

"You here, Baron!" she cried, apparently surprised. "That is lucky! I am just in need of a knight."

"Command me at your pleasure," replied the Baron.

"Why, that is quite self-understood; all you have to do is to obey. Now, then, Baron, I find this place charming, and as it is evening now, I will stay here over night, in order to see the sun rise. Fellow," she said to the hunter; "you may take this buck down to the village; keep the meat, but bring me the skin in the morning."

When the hunter had gone, the Baron

said: "That is a capital idea, your staying hear to see the sun rise; I was just about to propose that to you."

"Ah! but do you see these heavy boots, Baron? I cannot be withont my slippers; I must have my slippers."

"What is to be done?" the Baron asked, perplexed.

"That is very simple," said Antonette. "Go down into the village and fetch them."

"That is certainly very simple, ha, ha, ha! very simple, indeed — simple, indeed," the Baron laughed. It was a forced laugh, but Antonette would leave him no time.

"Go down and fetch them, and be quick about it. I am of an impatient disposition, and very hungry, — you hear, — very hungry."

That settled it. The Baron hastened down to the village, and after an hour or so returned with a pair of dainty bullion-embroidered slippers, fit for the feet of a princess.

"That was quick, Baron," cried Antonette. "You shall be royally rewarded for your obedience: I give you permission to put them on for me."

The Baron thought this really a royal reward, and was delighted. His delight increased when she slapped his hand for his awkwardness.

The Baron was a Hungarian magnate, and they never do things by halves. At his wink a man stepped into the room loaded with baskets, containing dainty viands and choice wines. And when Antonette set the table and arranged everything with housewifely grace, his exuberance of joy made him speechless. He sat in the chair and gazed at her, open-mouthed.

Having enjoyed their supper, they took seats outside of the cabin and gazed at the mountains, cañons, and the many picturesque Alpine villages, which the moonlight revealed.

Meantime, Antonette discoursed upon her tastes and peculiarities, which were sufficiently bizarre and eccentric to kindle the fire of love in his baronial breast. She culminated her eccentricity by rolling and smoking a cigarette. Before retiring into the shepherdess's cabin Antonette enjoined upon the Baron to call her early, so as not to miss that beautiful sight in the Alps, — a sunrise.

"Do you know, Baron," said Antonette the next morning, when she was ready to go home again, "I am very tired?"

"Shall I fetch a mule to carry you to the village?" the Baron asked.

"O no! what are you here for?" Antoinette said with a bewitching smile.

"Shall I carry you?"

"Certainly; I am sure it will make you happy to sigh under such a beautiful burden. You told me last night that I was beautiful."

"Beautiful!—ha, ha! you are more than beautiful. You are divine," cried the Baron, in ecstasy.

"This is better, still," said she. "Take, then, thy divinity, and carry her to her abode in the village."

The Baron saw no other way than to carry the beautiful girl upon his back. When they neared the village, Antonette commanded the Baron to halt. Stepping down, she arranged her dress, and, taking his arm, they walked into the village.

VIII.

"Good morning, Mrs. de Fallon. Is Madamoiselle, your daughter, in?"

"Ah, Herr Director Kraut! pray enter; I will call her at once."

Antonette made her appearance, before he had time to take stock of the furniture.

"Ah, see, the Director! How do you do?" she said, giving him her hand. She was not at all humble. She expected to see him this morning, because Seebag had brought her his play the day before, and that was on the day she and Ludmilla had returned to Vienna. The instructions of the latter had been minute.

"Just tell Seebag to send word to Director Kraut that he had written a play for you," Ludmilla had said. The result was as expected. The Director made his appearance.

"You are a witch to get that fellow Seebag to write you a play; why, he has persistently refused to write a line for us."

"Ah, my dear Director! I shall not appear in the part he has written. In fact, I shall never go on the stage again," said Antonette, sadly.

"Not appear in the role Seebag has written!" cried the Director, springing from his seat. "Not go on the stage again! Why? What is the matter? And this, now that Baron Zano, Seebag, and the Count are interested in you. Ye gods! are you insane?"

"No, Herr Director. But I recognize the futility of ever becoming a great actress. I doubt the soundness of my talent. Without a master, how could I possibly succeed? The interest of those three gentlemen is flattering, but it balances lightly against yours. Your interest in me would make of mediocrity a genius. Under your instruction I would have no doubts, and no anxiety about my success."

Her arms were stretched out toward him in supplication, while her face expressed sorrow, anxiety, and hope.

Now, as a matter of course, this was a bold demand on the part of Antonette. For the "royal and imperial Director Adolphus Kraut," as he was styled, could have commanded any price had he chosen to instruct aristocratic maidens in elocution. But he refused such offers, because he was rich, and occupied an honorable position under his sovereign. But Director Kraut was human; his heart followed the same impulse which sways the prince and the pauper, neither of whom is impervious against the power of love and beauty.

When Director Kraut heard the beautiful Antonette thus humbly pleading, his heart gave a leap in his fat bosom, and, springing from the chair, he fell on one knee before her.

"Adored Antonette!" he cried, "whose beauty has inspired the genius of a Seebag, and brought to your feet a Hungarian magnat,—I cannot resist you! Adored one! I will do as you desire; I will devote my time to your part. I will be your teacher, guide, slave, anything you desire! You shall — you must — become famous."

The light of joy and victory shone in her radiant eyes as she placed her alabaster-like hand upon his shoulder and begged him to rise. Gently he took her hand from off his shoulder and kissed it, and she let him hold it until the rustling of a silk dress announced the approach of Antonette's mother.

The fat Director sprang nimbly to his

chair, and folded his stubby little hands over his stomach, his face taking on an expression such as conscience-stricken children are wont to show after some naughty act.

Having been told of his praiseworthy intention, Antonette's mother was profuse in her thanks to the dear Herr Director.

"Only the dear Lord in Heaven can reward you for such a noble act," said Madame de Fallon.

"I should hate to wait for it," was the Director's mental rejoinder; but he was careful not to express it. After appointing an hour for the reading of her part, he kissed Antonette's hand with the utmost deference, bowed to the mamma, and left.

Half an hour later, Ludmilla came to the house. Being told by Antonette how she had managed the Director, Ludmilla said·—

"I think you will succeed; and now for the last cipher in the principle of the 'rule of four,' the great and only Dr. Grau."

IX.

A week had passed since the Director had first visited Antonette. He had kept his appointment with regularity, and sank deeper and deeper into the love-meshes of the beautiful actress. His instruction was a revelation, and Antonette, who by no means lacked talent, filled the Director with wonder and admiration. He promised her a great future.

Believing the time ripe for figuring with the cipher which went by the name of Dr. Grau, Antonette sent him a polite note to call on her.

Knowing the character of the man she was to deal with, she dressed — to harmonize with the fated part she was to play—in a gown of black silk trimmed with black velvet. The room was darkened, and everything looked somber and ghostly. Upon her writing-desk was a skull and a revolver. Everything looked so gruesome that the great Dr. Grau involuntarily shivered when he was shown into Antonette's room.

She received him with quiet dignity. Her face seemed inexpressibly sad; the white frill around her neck, contrasting with the black gown and the black lace upon her head, made her face pale. An indefinable gloom seemed to hover about her beautiful mouth, and her smile spoke of patient resignation.

Dr. Grau contemplated her features, and thought that he had never seen anything so beautiful and classical. He had heard of Seebag's play, "The Fated Star," and when she asked his opinion, the great critic felt pleased and flattered.

"An author may write a play, an actress might attempt its interpretation, but towering over both stands the critic," said she. "His judgment is supreme; it is the only guide."

In her conversation she displayed so much pessimism, that the great critic was shocked.

"Believe me, dear Doctor," she said, sadly, "if it were not for my art, I would have made an end of this life long ago. Oh, how often have I pressed this revolver against my temple to do it!"

"For heaven's sake," cried Dr. Grau, "it would be a crime to rob the world of such a genius, such a philosophical spirit, which is sure to revive art and give our stage the stamp of greatness. I shall take this revolver with me." Slipping the weapon into his pocket, he continued: "I could not sleep in peace as long as this weapon was on your desk."

"You are right; take it along," said Antonette, sadly. "But you take from me only the mechanical means of ending this life. You must do more,— if you would save me, dear Doctor, you must become the physician of my soul. Come to me often. In a spiritual intercourse with you, I may regain the lost joy of life."

When the great critic left Antonette, his head was in a whirl; he admired her as much as the author of "The Fated Star," the eccentric Baron, and the convivial Director.

X.

The "Ring Theater," in Vienna, was filled with people, and hundreds upon hundreds were turned away, unable to gain admission. Director Kraut had foreseen that the "Burg Theater" would not be adequate to the demand for seats by the aristocracy and the *haute finance*, let alone the people; and he arranged the presentation of "The Fated Star" at the more commodious "Ring Theater."

But the beauty of the new star, whose pictures were to be seen in every shop window, and for whom the famous Seebag had especially written "The Fated Star," attracted all classes of society in the "Kaiserstadt."

In one of the proscenium boxes sat Ludmilla Lassen, surrounded by four gentlemen. Her face beamed with pleasure as she gazed upon the vast audience, — that brilliant array of beauty, refinement, and wealth. But suddenly her brow clouded; she grew silent, and seemed strangely nervous.

"One would think that this was your *début*, you are so pale and nervous, beautiful Ludmilla," said Baron Zano.

"I don't know how it is, but I do feel distressed and nervous just now," Ludmilla replied.

Director Kraut uttered a loud laugh. "Never fear, Ludi; she will take the house by storm."

"If she preserve her dignity before the audience as she has done hitherto, there can be no doubt of her success," said Dr. Grau, sententiously.

Seebag alone seemed to share Ludmilla's nervousness, but he said nothing.

The rythmic tones of one of Strauss's waltzes, especially arranged for the occasion, put the friends of Antonette de Fallon in better humor. The tremendous applause was taken as a good omen; but when the storm of applause had subsided,

Ludmilla's nervousness returned, and, driven by an unconquerable anxiety, she rose and announced her intention of going to Antonette's room.

"She might want my assistance," Ludmilla said.

"I would not go, if I were you," said Dr. Grau; "she will do very well,—if no unforeseen misfortune is brought about by the people in the cast."

Hardly had he uttered the last words, when two huge flames were seen shooting up from the footlights. In an instant the curtain was one sheet of fire. A cry of despair rose above the vast audience. It came from beneath the stage, and for a moment all was silent. Then ensued a scene such as is beyond human power to describe. One impulse seemed to sway all. They rose, and, gazing at the leaping flames, were transfixed with horror. The pale faces, the rigid bodies, seemed petrified. Soon, however, the reaction set in; they turned as if with one accord, and made a rush for the door.

Had there been no impediment, they might have gradually left the house. But women had fainted, and the men who bent down to assist them were instantly crushed down and trampled on. However, the momentary and minute opening was immediately closed as if by a vice. Nature's most brutal maxim is that which expresses the law of self-preservation, and of all animals, the human is the most brutal advocate and executor. In the theater, big men were seen to put their hands on the shoulders of weak women, and thus lift themselves up, seeking to gain exit and possible safety. The weaker victims broke down with a shriek, that was drowned under the feet of those who profited by the temporary opening. Frantic men and women leaped from the balcony and landed on the heads of those below, whose necks they broke, while others positively walked on the heads of that trampled, despairing mass of humanity. A few daring ones saved themselves by leaping from high windows.

At the door, which unfortunately opened from within, the horrors were ghastly in the extreme. The awful catastrophe seemed to have robbed many of their reason.

"Open the doors! Open the doors!" they shrieked. "You are keeping the doors closed on purpose to burn us alive!" They cursed the "Fated Star" and its author, they cursed God and the Emperor, and with blood-curdling yells fastened their teeth in the cheeks of those against whom they were pitched, in the agony of unrelenting fate. And now ensued a scene, the ghastliness of which surpasses expression. They tore each others' flesh, biting, biting, till their heads fell against each other, dead.

At length the doors were broken, and those nearest fell in the doorway; the dying were trampled to death. Like a gigantic wave, the mass of tortured humanity rushed into the aperture where the stairs were leading down into the hall, and instantly the funnel-shaped opening was clogged with dead and dying.

Among those who escaped with their lives were the Director, Dr. Grau, — the latter a raving maniac, — Seebag, and Ludmilla. Her hair had turned completely white, but she was more composed than Seebag, who wept like a child, and seemed broken in spirit and body. "I have lost all, all," he cried; "everything that makes life worth living. Antonette, Antonette, you were the 'Fated Star,'—my 'Fated Star.'"

Ludmilla supported him as they made their way through the populace. The tears ran down her pallid cheeks.

"I have calculated without fate," she murmured.

A CHRISTMAS PROMISE.

I.

"*EHRE sei Gott in der Hoehe, und Friede auf Erden, und den Menschen ein Wohlgefallen.*"

"Glory be to God in the highest, and peace on earth and good will to man."

Some one had opened the door of the church on the Friedrichs Platz, in Berlin, and the words quoted rang out into the silent square, clear and distinct. Opposite the church, in the "Platz," that was covered by a foot and a half of snow, but which had been cleared in places for pedestrians, a lady and a gentleman, both dressed in elegant furs, their feet in high goloshes, walked up and down. They were young, and the lady was very beautiful. She was a blonde, and her cloak and head-covering, the latter in the shape of the national Polish "chapka," were of blue velvet trimmed with silver fox. Needless to say that this enhanced her beauty, which was classical. Her companion was of medium height, of dark complexion, and mobile-featured. People might have called him homely, but no one would have passed him without turning the head to take another glance at the retreating form. The remarkable feature in the gentleman's make-up was his eyes. Heavens! what eyes he had! One might have read all the passions in them, but not stupidity. For Nathan Berger's eyes were the *Eyes of Genius*. They were jet black, and one could see every object mirrored in their spectrum.

When he heard the words coming from

the church, he gazed at the edifice, then at his companion, and said:

"In there they sing about 'peace on earth.' They lie! there is no peace on earth, Sophie," he cried, taking hold of the girl's arm. "Give me peace; give me rest. The yellow leaves, which the autumn winds have blown from these trees, are buried beneath the snow,— they are at rest; they have peace. Ah! but— who knows?" he said, as if soliloquizing,—" maybe some worm is gnawing their dry carcasses; then there is no peace for them, either. Sophie, do you love me as I love you? Tell me!"

"I love you more than any one on earth, Nathan; but—"

"But," he cried, when Sophie hesitated, — "but you find it impossible to marry me, because your parents are against it. Do you remember, love, when I first played in Leipsic? When I first looked into your beauteous face, — ah! then I played for you only. You were my inspiration. My mind was unconscious of my playing, because my soul was with you, and my bow was guided by the hands of an angel. Ah, dear love! how I must have played to cause so much enthusiasm among the people! — and yet I was utterly oblivious of their existence. For me no one existed but you, love. And now it is all over with me; I cannot play any more; my violin weeps, — it weeps, weeps, weeps."

"*Und Friede auf Erden,*" came from the church again.

"And peace on earth!" he mocked. "Idiots! don't you see that it is all a farce? There is no peace, I tell you. I have come all the way from America to your land of music and learning. I was a child of nature. I loved God, my parents, and my violin, and — I had peace. It is but six months since I came here, and I am stranded. My peace is gone,—because I love hopelessly." The last word was almost a sob.

Sophie leaned her head on his shoulder, and her tears trickled down upon his fur. The brilliancy of the tears caught his eye.

"Don't cry, dear love,—Sophie, dear, don't cry," he said, forgetting his own anguish at the sight of hers. "Is there no way out of this difficulty? Come with me to America. My parents will love you as they love me."

"And have a father's curse upon my life; break my mother's heart. Oh! Nathan dear, wait; maybe father will relent. We are young,—we can afford to wait a couple of years."

"Ah," said Nathan, "time cures or kills. In a couple of years from now, I may be dead, and you—married."

"Never!" cried Sophie. "I will never marry any one but you. Wait, darling, for my sake."

"I will," said he. "I will wait for you. I will hope — and with your promise it will not be — against hope. But I will never live to see you married to any one else. Men of my character love but once, and die."

His dark brow contracted threateningly; his eyes flashed fire, but it was for a moment only, and as the church door opened again, and the song of the Christmas anthem reached his ear, — "Und Friede auf Erden," — he was not bitter against the glorious promise. He pressed Sophie's hand to his heart. "We may yet have peace and happiness," he said.

"Amen," the girl responded, and as the people left the church they mingled with the crowd, and were lost to view.

II.

"What sweeter promise can possibly be made to mankind than the one which the angel brought to the lowly of Palestine, 'Behold, I bring you tidings of great joy'? This promise of great joy is the birth of Christ," ran the preacher's sermon in the church on the Friedrichs Platz. "Who would not rejoice at such a promise? For we know that the Father will keep His promise of giving to the world His only begotten Son. It is in our hearts to believe it. For are not we — weak and sinful though we be — eager to keep our promises given to those we love? and we rejoice at the joy we shall give to those who expect the fulfillment of our sacred promises." As he uttered the last sentence, a sob was heard that rose and seemed to flutter through the vast building. Some of the worshipers turned to see whence it came.

In the center of the aisle sat Herr Marlow, a stout and choleric-looking gentleman, his wife, and his daughter Sophie; the latter was weeping. By her side sat a young man, elegantly dressed, who bent over her and whispered in her ear. Instinctively she drew away from him; he seemed amazed, and his low forehead contracted; he looked at Herr Marlow; the latter shrugged his shoulders and listened to the sermon.

"Are you ill, Miss Marlow?" said the young man by her side.

She made no answer.

"Are you weeping for that fiddler?" hissed Mrs. Marlow in Sophie's ear. "I will tell your father as soon as we get home," the mother threatened. At this moment the preacher said "Amen!" and the congregation rose.

The organ pealed forth a grand overture, and as Mr. and Mrs. Marlow were nearing the door the former stumbled and fell. Mrs. Marlow screamed, and Sophie stood as if petrified. A great commotion ensued; every one wanted to know what had happened. A physician made his way to where Mr. Marlow lay; he looked at the prostrate man, who was blue in the face, his eyes staring into vacancy, and a white film on his lips. The physician placed his hand on the man's breast, rose, and said, "Apoplexy." Mrs. Marlow's lamentations were heart-rending. "Dead, dead!" she cried.

The well-dressed young man put his arm around Sophie's waist, but she pushed him away, and threw herself by her father's side. "Oh, father, father," she cried, "what an unhappy lot is mine!"

"Sophie, dear Sophie," breathed some

one by her side. Sophie did not turn, she knew the voice; it was Nathan Berger. A shiver ran through her frame, and, forgetting the world and all around her, she laid her head on his breast and wept. All of a sudden Mrs. Marlow's voice was heard, shrill and unforgiving, "Leave us, please," she cried.

Nathan Berger rose without a word and left the church. As he passed by the well-dressed young man, the latter threw him a look of malicious hatred. "We don't need your fiddle here, Herr Berger," he hissed. Nathan Berger never turned. He thought that it was just one year since Sophie Marlow had promised to be his, — hoping that her father would give in. He now decided to wait another year.

III.

"If he should wake while I am away," said Dr. Wagner to the young man at the bedside, "just give him a teaspoonful of this medicine. The crisis is over; he will pull through. But be careful not to let him have any excitement; no one is to be admitted. I will be here again this afternoon.

On the bed, pale and haggard, lay Nathan Berger. On his lips played a happy smile, as he repeatedly uttered the name "Sophie." . . . .

Suddenly he opened his eyes, — his glorious eyes had not lost their luster. It was ten o'clock in the morning; the bells from the steeple in the neighborhood called the people to the worship of the annually newly born joy, — the birth of Christ. Nathan asked no questions, — he knew that it was Christmas. He recalled Sophie's promise, two years previous, to be his, and then the announcement of her engagement to Dr. Pille. He remembered clearly the reading of the paragraph; how each word and each letter had cut his heart and had fallen like molten lead upon his soul. Then all had grown dark; he knew no more until he awoke this morning. He thought that he must have fainted, and that his friend had put him to bed.

It was about time to rise; he had an appointment to play at the Academy. He wanted to get out of bed, but was quite unable to move a limb.

"Keep perfectly quiet, Nat," said his friend. "Here, take this medicine and try to sleep. The doctor will be here again this afternoon."

"How is that?" said Nathan Berger. "Have I been ill?"

"Yes, very," his friend replied. "We have despaired of your life; but you pulled through, like a good fellow, and now, if you will behave properly, you will soon be able to be about again."

"Have I been ill long?" asked Berger, astonished.

"About six weeks," said the other.

Nathan sighed and turned his face to the wall, without making any remark. When his friend smoothed the pillow and asked Nathan to try and sleep, the latter turned his face, and the young man saw the luminous eyes suffused with tears.

IV.

They stood in a row for blocks and blocks on Mission Street, in San Francisco, each one eager to buy a ticket for the "*Berger Concert.*" Patti, in her most palmy days, could not have boasted of such an enthusiastic throng. Berger had played at the Metropolitan Temple, and his violin had set the music-loving San Francisco people wild with enthusiasm. "He is crazy," said some. "He is a genius," others said. But men and women broke down and wept at the tremendous heartache that burst forth from his instrument. And for weeks his playing had been discussed in the street, in clubs, and in the parlor. The announcement of a concert at the Grand Opera House, therefore, brought all sorts and conditions of people to Mission Street. They stood in the pelting rain, heedless of cold and inconvenience. Two doors from the entrance to the theater stood a woman dressed in black and heavily veiled. She had been in line nearly an hour; her teeth chattered, and she seemed faint. A gentleman by her side, observing her pitiful condition, at first wondered that people could be so "music mad" as to endanger their lives. He spoke to her, telling her to go home, as she would be ill. But she merely said: "I must have a ticket."

Then, out of sheer pity, he placed his broad form in front of her, so as to shield her from the rain. He was a gentleman! And when he was near the box-office he took her money and bought her ticket. She thanked him and entered the Grand Opera House.

V.

..... Nathan Berger's appearance was greeted with tremendous applause. He did not seem to notice it. His pale face was impassive; but his eyes, those luminous orbs, searched the vast audience as an astronomer the skies, and when the uproar had subsided, he took his violin, placed it in position, and with a sweep of his bow played a symphony. It was a masterful rendition. But all of a sudden he stopped, — stopped just for a moment, — and then there were heard those plaintive sounds as of weeping angels. They grew in intensity and volume. They spread over the vast house, and fell upon the hearers as the forebodings of a tremendous calamity. Then there was heard a sigh that fluttered above the people and mingled with those sorrowful strains, and as Nathan Berger drew out his bow in one prolonged tone of agony, all the strings of the violin snapped with a loud report. In the audience a cry was heard, and Nathan Berger fell upon the stage in a faint. Unspeakable confusion ensued. Women became hysterical, and men rushed upon the stage to assist as much as possible. Some one in the audience called for a doctor, — a woman had fainted. The doctor was on hand. It was the woman in black; she was pale as death, but her features, though worn, were of exquisite beauty. "She is dead," said the doctor. She was at once conveyed to the receiving hospital, because the doctor might be mistaken, as some thought. But she was dead; she had died of heart failure. In her pocket was found an elegant card-case, with black-rimmed cards, which bore the inscription: —

"Frau Dr. Sophie Pille,
Wittwe,
18 Spandauer Strasse,
Berlin, W."

She was buried by the German pastor three days later, and his text was, "Ehre sei Gott in der Hoehe, und Friede auf Erden, und den Menschen ein Wohlgefallen."

It was Christmas!

THE STORY OF VLADIMIR.

"SAY, Burton, what has become of that tall Russian friend of yours with the elegant furs and patent leather topboots?" said Anderson, a young American, who studied medicine at the University of Heidelberg.

"He is dead," replied Gustave Burton, a fellow-student.

"Died in his boots, I suppose?" said the American.

"No, he died of a broken heart," the other replied.

"Well, that is romantic,— a vicious Nihilist to die of a broken heart. He died, at least, in Siberia?" queried Anderson.

"It would have been in the general fitness of things."

Burton seemed hurt at the sarcasm, and said: "He was worthy of a better fate; he was a noble fellow, and, far from being a vicious Nihilist, he was an enthusiast, courageous and refined."

"He certainly was very handsome," said Anderson. "Do you mind telling me what caused his death?"

"His story is best told in his letters," Burton replied.

"I should very much like to read them," said Anderson.

Burton unlocked a metal box, from which he took a package of letters tied with a black ribbon

"Here they are," said he. "Read them and judge of the young man's character. He was not a Nihilist when he was here, nor was he acquainted with the leaders of the Propaganda. And when he went to Russia he said that he did not care sufficiently for politics to bother about them. It seems, however, that Professor Herten, a friend of his father, took him in hand and initiated him in the mysteries of the social agitation. His first letters speak in the most glowing terms about the professor; the most interesting are the two last."

Anderson opened one of them and read:—

I.

"Dear Gustave,— Six months have elapsed since I wrote you last. What a change these six months have wrought in my life! I have lost my passiveness for politics and—my equilibrium. I am in a constant fever of excitement. What I have seen surpasses description. Such misery! Such ignorance! Such brutality! And we

. still live! — live in abundance and affluence; enjoy all the seeming blessings which education allots us. But there is really no blessing in it at all; for we have no sooner learned to appreciate life, than we are appalled at the awful misery which surrounds us.

"But let me thank God for the privilege of being permitted to write to you again. You will shudder to think how near I came to being prevented from indulging in such a pleasure. I had been sent to St. Petersburg, and on my arrival was met at the depot by two gentlemen, one tall and stately, and the other of medium height, and swarthy-looking. The tall gentleman gave me the sign; but I hesitated to recognize him, because I thought I had seen the other gentleman enter the car I had been in, at a way-station. I was not quite sure, but it was sufficient to keep me on my guard. And yet his features were not at all repulsive or suspicious-looking. In fact, they looked so much like one who was near and dear to me, that the similarity was astonishing. But this man with the black, glossy hair and whiskers and dark complexion, I was sure was quite a different person. While I was thus hesitating a smile flitted across his face.

"'We had better take a carriage and carry off Vladimir, without delay.'

"The sound of his voice caused me a faintness of heart. I was about to make an exclamation, but a sharp look bade me be silent. In the carriage I could not master myself any longer. I threw my arms around the dark man's neck. 'Herten,' I cried with a sob, 'dear Herten!'

"It was the professor. His make-up was so perfect that I did not recognize him.

"'We were uneasy about you,' said he, 'and I thought it best to be on hand. I have to be in Moscow in a week. You will stay at Romanov's house while here.'

"Romanov was the tall gentleman. But I did not enjoy long his hospitality, having been arrested that very evening. Romanov occupied an elegant mansion on the Nevsky Prospect. After our arrival at the mansion, we were brought to our rooms, bathed, and shortly after dined. After dinner the professor attended to his correspondence, Romanov went out, and I left the mansion, with the intention of looking around town.

"Not far from the Nevsky Prospect is a magnificent square, in the center of which is a small lake surrounded by artificial grottos. In one of these sat a gentleman, reading. I seated myself in the same grotto, took a French newspaper from my pocket, and began to read. I saw that my companion was scrutinizing me, and, somewhat annoyed, I turned around, struck a match and lit a cigar. He arose, and, coming up to me, politely asked for a light for his cigarette, addressing me in French. He was very amiable, and, seating himself by my side, said that he was a Frenchman and glad to have found a countryman. I told him that I was not a Frenchman, but had learned the French language from my father, who was of French descent and spoke the language fluently.

"'May I take the liberty of inquiring his name?' said he, in a very winning way. 'Pardon me,' he added, gracefully, 'that I have not told you my name; I am called Lenier,—Charles François Lenier.'

"'You are very kind,' said I; 'my father's name was Pierre Vladislav.'

"What was it that passed over his face? It contracted as if in great pain; but this was only momentary; for when I asked him if he was ill, he looked at me with a pleasant smile.

"'Ah! it is nothing but that troublesome gout, which occasionally gets hold of me. It is over now. Do you intend to remain long at the capital?'

"'A few weeks,' said I. This ended the conversation; he bowed and left the grotto.

"On reflection, I was not quite pleased with that Frenchman. I had certainly no business to tell him my name. Putting the paper into my pocket I left the grotto, and turned toward the Nevsky Prospect. But had not gone twenty paces when two gendarmes placed their hands on my shoulders and arrested me in the name of the Czar.

. . . .
. . . .

"'So you are Vladimir, the son of Pierre Vladislav,' said the pseudo-Frenchman, who was none other than the Inspector of Police.

"'I am,' said I.

"'Do you know where you are now?'

"'I suppose in the fortress Peter-Paul.'

"'Exactly.'

"'And what do you want of me?'

"'I want you to tell me what object you have in coming to St. Petersburg, when you are a student in Moscow and have no vacation?'

"I was silent.

"'Who came with you?'

"Still no answer.

"'At whose house do you stop?'

"I remained silent.

"'Answer, you dog, as I have the means to make you talk,' he cried.

"His superficial politeness was all gone; he was a Tartar.

"'You may have the means to torture

THE STORY OF VLADIMIR. 103

me,' said I, 'but you have none to make me talk. I shall say no more.'

"'You shall, you cursed dog. I will see whether your flesh is as tough as your character; but, before I go on, let me tell you that you may choose between the mines of Siberia and a life of pleasure. Give me the name of the rebels in Moscow and here, and you shall be set free, protected by me. You are young, possess talent, and we can use talented and loyal servants. Choose!'

"I said nothing.

"At a motion of the Inspector's hand, a Cossack, evidently used to such scenes, took off my coat and stripped me to the waist. Another motion and my hands and feet were tied, and I was placed on a long bench.

"'You have still time,' said my executioner.

"But I kept silent.

"How can I describe their fiendish brutality? My back was cut to the bone by the knout. Consciousness was about leaving me, when I felt a sponge pressed to my lips, a cold shiver passed through my body, and all was dark.

"When I awoke to consciousness again, I looked into the face of Professor Herten.

"'Where am I?' I said, feebly.

"'With me, Vladimir.'

"'But how came I here?' I asked, as the remembrance of what I had suffered gradually came back to me.

"'When you were arrested, I was but a few steps from you. Discretion demanded my non-interference. You could not escape the clutches of the police then, but I could save you afterwards. I was apprised of your fate by the physician, who is an old friend of mine. It was he who pressed the saturated sponge to your month, while holding your pulse, and pronounced you dead. You were left with instructions to be buried. As soon as you feel strong enough, we will leave for Moscow, although you need not fear the "late" Police Inspector any more.'

"'What! Did you say "late"? Is he no longer in his position?'

"'Better than that,—he is dead!'

"I was quite overcome. Dead! He who had witnessed my father's sufferings and torn the flesh from my bones. Surely he deserved death; but I did not think it would overtake him so quickly.

"The professor handed me a newspaper, wherein it was stated that the Police Inspector had been assassinated in bed. I could not read any further. The letters danced before my eyes. I swooned away.

. . . .

"I am again in Moscow, and but few know of my existence, as the police would be only too glad to make me an object of their earnest consideration. I live in different quarters, bear a different name, and not one — not even my mother — would know me by my appearance.

"Adieu.

"Ever your affectionate

"Vladimir."

II.

"Berne, Switzerland, May 1, 1883.

"My Dear Gustave, — Some time has elapsed since you last heard from me. I have been on the highest pinnacle of bliss, and have fallen into the deepest deep of despair. In this happy country, where liberty is the heirloom of every child, I am comparatively free, — that is, I am not harassed by the police. But alas! I shall not live long to enjoy life, as the physicians have declared my malady incurable. Indeed, they could cure or attempt to cure every known disease; but is there a cure for a broken heart? I am therefore prepared for the worst. Worst! —did I say worst? Well, I retract that expression; death to me has nothing terrible. It will redeem me from my misery, and I ought to contemplate its approach with the satisfaction we accord a friend. Although the recital of my sad experience causes me intense pain, yet I know that in your heart there is a responsive chord for the sorrows of a friend.

"It was in the forenoon of a bleak November day, 1880, I was at my desk writing, that Professor Herten entered and told me that I was to leave for St. Petersburg at once.

"'Be cautious and quick,' he said. 'The reports are very disquieting. The firebrands Hartman and Russiakoff are brewing mischief, and that crazy Petrovsky is backing them with money. There is but one man whose influence can do some good, Count Datleff. We are watched, and you must try all means to get them to desist. If they do not, it will spoil the work of years. No extremes!'

"Receiving money and a passport, I left that night for St. Petersburg. There my message caused a flurry among those who had a desire to see bloodshed. A letter from Datleff, that arrived simultaneously with me, cautioned not to make any attempt that was liable to double the vigilance and activity of the police. I was ordered to take a message to Datleff at once, but to take the *chaussée* instead of the railroad. This command somewhat surprised me. If the message was so pressing, why was I to take a slower means of conveyance? I expressed myself to that effect; they gave me the reason of the trains being watched, etc., and I was forced to go by the post-chaise. I reached the village of K—— without any mishap, and, being very tired, I asked the post-master to show me a room where I could rest until about to resume my journey. He conducted me to a pleasant room, and in a few moments I was fast asleep.

"I was roughly aroused, and looking about me, saw three Cossacks at my bedside.

"One of them, a corporal, ordered me to get up immediately. I jumped up, and, without asking any questions, followed them. Resistance on my part would have been madness, for it would have resulted in death. I had to deliver a message to Datleff, and, who knows, an opportunity for escape might offer itself on the road. They handcuffed and put me in a 'troyka,' where I sat between the corporal and one of the

Cossacks, both holding their carbines on their knees ready to fire, while the third Cossack drove the horses. I had never experienced such a drive. The horses raced as if driven by furies; it almost took my breath away. Suddenly we came to a bend in the road, and before the maddened horses could be turned, the 'troyka' dashed against a tree. We were literally lifted from the vehicle and thrown into the compact snow, while the team fell into a deep ditch. It was marvelous that none of us was hurt except the driver, who was stunned, but revived in a few minutes. The corporal and one of the Cossacks looked after the team. The 'troyka' was broken beyond repair, one of the horses had been killed, and two were extracted after the traces had been cut. The corporal and one of the Cossacks mounted each a horse, while the third drove me in front of them.

It was quite dark when we reached one of those monjick huts so frequently found in the Russian steppes. The horses being tired, and my guardians hungry, they lost no time in getting under shelter.

"'Hey, monjick! Hay for my horses, and vodky for us,' cried the corporal, as he entered the hut.

"'None to spare, Cossack,' replied the peasant.

"The corporal, infuriated at this curt reply, rushed at the peasant; but at that moment his young wife appeared with a light in her hand. The corporal stepped back, bewildered by her beauty.

"But I could have screamed with joy, for in that peasant's wife I recognized Katinka, the beautiful daughter of old Cahileff, one of my father's tenants. The recognition was mutual, but an almost imperceptible motion of her lips told me to keep quiet. Oh! I was quite sure Katinka would save me, and with a light heart I sat down upon a three-legged stool by the fire.

"'What do you wish, sir?' she asked, in a sweet voice.

"'I want some hay for my horses, *gospodyinna* (madam).'

"'Ivan, give the corporal some hay, while I prepare some soup,' said she to her husband.

"Ivan said, '*Harasho*' (very well), and left the room, accompanied by one of the soldiers. While Ivan and the soldier were outside attending to the horses, Katinka put a stone jug with whisky on the table, and told the Cossacks to help themselves. They needed no second invitation, and very soon their natural tendency toward singing asserted itself. They sang one of those plaintive songs, full of longing for their homes and sweethearts. Ivan's wife, too, sang a German song. But if the Cossacks had understood the meaning of those words I doubt not but that they would have cut her down in spite of her beauty.

"'Behind the house,' sang she, 'to the right, stands my cousin's saddled horse. He is asleep upstairs. When the soldiers are deep in whisky, then, dear Vladimir, take the horse and ride a mile on the road until you come to a white house. There my uncle lives; he will save you.'

"In the mean time Ivan and the Cossack returned; they seemed on the best of terms. The Cossack introduced Ivan to the corporal as an old acquaintance, and all drank *vodky*.

"The corporal found the vodky salubrious for his temper; he offered me some vodky, and at Katinka's solicitation removed my fetters. Soon the steaming soup was served; but, hungry as I was, I could eat nothing, my mind being on the venture I was to make. Seated between the Cossacks, I made every attempt to swallow a spoonful of the soup; but I was trembling with agitation, and my teeth chattered against the tin spoon as often as I put it into my mouth. If the Cossacks had divined my thoughts, there is hardly any doubt but that I would not have been in a position now to write this story.

"But the human mind is a mysterious world of its own, and hence I was permitted to brood deliriously over my plans of escape while the Cossacks tranquilly ate their supper. Suddenly a sound was heard from without, that froze the blood in our veins.

"It was the howl of wolves and the dying shriek of a horse torn to pieces by those terrible beasts, that abound in the Russian steppes only.

"'The horses!' cried Ivan and the Cossacks simultaneously, and Ivan rushed to the door.

"'Take your rifle,' cried Katinka.

"'I'll go with you,' said the corporal.

"'And so will I,' added one of the Cossacks.

"They rushed out, and I was left alone with one Cossack. Katinka, being a Russian woman, knew that a political prisoner would as lief face wolves in his attempt to gain liberty as to go to Siberia. She therefore cried in German: 'Now or never!'

"I can scarcely describe what happened in the next few moments. My hand still trembles; my mind gets confused, and I have to close my eyes and pause when I think of it. Quick as a flash, I jumped up, grasped the stone jug and struck the Cossack a blow on the head; he fell like a log. Snatching the pistols from his belt, and telling Katinka to cry for help after a few minutes, so as to free her from the suspicion of aiding in my escape, I ran from the room.

"I found the saddled horse, and, firing one of the pistols as a signal, I soon heard Katinka cry for help.

"It was a race for life. In a few minutes I was at the house of Katinka's uncle. When the latter heard who I was, he said: 'Don't stop here! You are lost if you do. The Cossacks will surely be here shortly. Take a fresh horse and ride direct to Badin Castle; it is a straight road. You cannot miss it. It is eighty *vierst*. You will get there by ten or eleven o'clock tomorrow morning. Don't spare the horse; he is strong.'

"A few minutes later I was on my way

to Badin Castle, which I reached at noon the next day.

"Count Datleff, the gentleman to whom I was to deliver an awful message was about forty-five years of age. He was six feet in height, finely proportioned, and very handsome of features. He was in his study, — a spacious apartment, the walls showing a fine library. The table was covered with maps and papers. Addressing me, he said : —

"'So you are Vladislav's son? Your father was a brave man,' he added with a far-off look. Then, after a moment : 'Can you imagine who was the cause of your arrest?'

"'I cannot,' I answered.

"'It was evidently a *ruse* to keep you from delivering the message,' he said. As if speaking to himself, he continued : 'They don't send plain Cossacks to arrest political suspects. Ah !' he cried ; 'it is so, it must be so. They sent word to the police that you are one of the men who committed the church robbery. Ha ! ha ! ha !' he laughed. 'That is quite a tumble down from your political pinnacle, young man ! You were merely arrested as a church-robber. *Tres bien!* The Cossacks will be sent to the mines for permitting you to escape. But you are here. I dare say they would roast those fellows alive, if they knew what bird slipped through their fingers. Well, thrice welcome, sir ! What is the message ?'

"As he uttered the last word, his face grew somber; and well it might, for I uttered an awful word. 'DEATH,' I said.

"When he heard that word he jumped from his seat, and laying his powerful hand on my shoulder, said, in a voice of thunder:—

"'Is that their message to me ? Are you sure you make no mistake?' He was fearful in his passion. However, I repeated the word.

"'No,' he cried; 'no blood. I don't want it. We are not assassins. We want rights and justice, but these are not the means to get them. In order to get a constitutional government, they would murder —'

"'Sir,' said I, 'we are not alone.'

"Between the curtains leading to another apartment stood a girl whose transcendent beauty surpasses expression; but she was pale and trembling. I had perceived her just as the last words had passed Count Datleff's lips. At my remark, he turned around, and seeing the girl, he extended his arms, saying: —

"'Eveline, my child, what do you wish?'

"She came to his arms, rested her head upon his shoulder, and, looking up to him, said with ineffable sweetness: —

"'My father!'

"There was a world of meaning in those two words. They told him that she was willing to help him bear his sorrow. How can I describe the beauty of the scene? It was the most divine sight my eyes had ever beheld. He, tall and strong, in his face supreme sorrow, in his sigh, broken hopes, suppressed anger, and with his arm encircling the form of a woman that in its frailness and pliancy seemed to me that of a supernatural being.

"When her father introduced her as his only child, I could find no words. I could make no remark in ordinary language. All that I might have said seemed to me, at that moment, banal and evanescent.

"She gave me her hand, smooth as alabaster. I touched the rosy tips of her fingers with my lips.

"'Eveline, my child,' said her father, 'I

will leave you here with my young friend
Vladimir. I shall return in a couple of
hours. I trust you will be friends.' He
kissed Eyeline on the forehead, and left.

"I cannot repeat what we talked about.
Two hours had passed as swiftly as two
seconds. Oh, most heavenly seconds! and
when her father returned, I knew that my
fate was sealed, that I loved Eveline with
all the might of my soul, — that her image
was indelibly stamped in my heart, and
that, had she bid me die, I should have
considered it divine bliss.

"'You are friends,' said her father, seeing our beaming faces. 'I am glad of that.
Leave us now, dear. We will dine in half
an hour.'

"My instructions were given to me with
a clearness and precision characteristic of
the man.

"'The train for Moscow leaves in two

hours. Go at once to Professor Herten and tell him my orders are: "No Blood!" We have not sunk so deeply as to murder a man who has done much good in his time, and, but for bad counsel, might have done better. The conquest of popular ignorance must precede popular liberty. If we educate the Russian people, they will liberate themselves; but let not the assassin think he can accomplish it.'

"Shortly after dinner I left for Moscow. Herten was delighted to see me. He doubted if Datleff's message would have any influence at this late hour. I do not know if he was disobeyed, or if his message was delivered at all. A few weeks later the world was shocked at the regicide committed by brutal assassins and furthered by misguided visionaries. A week later I went to Berlin.

"I had left Russia with conflicting feelings in my heart. Count Datleff's life, so noble and precious, was in imminent danger; and who could tell but that the one I prized above all things on earth might share her father's fate? My sorrow and anxiety increased, as days and weeks passed without any intelligence from Count Datleff. I could control myself no longer. I must go to her.

"I left Berlin for Moscow, the danger scarcely less than my intense longing to see Eveline. I arrived at Badin Castle three days later. The door opened, and I stood face to face with Eveline.

"When the confusion incident to my unexpected arrival had passed, she told me of the mental suffering her father had endured since I had gone. Her father, she said, had an idea that I was in England; and now I had come back to the lion's den.

"'Why did you come?' she said.

'They have been hunting for you in every house. You are in great danger.'

"I was silent, and listened to that sweet voice, which thrilled my soul.

"'I came,' I managed to articulate,— 'I came to see you. I believed your father and yourself in danger.'

"'And why do you wish to suffer with our misfortune? Go and save yourself.'

"'Never!'

"'Why?'

"'Because I love you; because I would suffer everything to save your sweet life.'

"As I spoke, she turned pale and pressed her hand to her heart.

"'Eveline, dear Eveline!' I cried; 'pardon me if I have hurt you; but my heart is surcharged with love, — one great love for you, my darling, my dear love! I have loved you from the moment I first saw you. Oh, tell me that I have not hurt you. Give me some hope; tell me that I may love you, — you alone.'

"I looked at her face, suffused with tears and smiles, and I sank on my knees. 'Eveline, my love!' I cried. She took my head in her hands.

"'Vladimir, dearest Vladimir,' she breathed. I caught her in my arms; and thus we stood, united in one great love, her head on my breast, her eyes closed, pale as a lily. Nor did we hear the opening of the door until the tall figure of the Count stood before us.

"'Vladimir! Eveline!' said he, smiling; he did not seem surprised at seeing me. Involuntarily we sank on our knees before the man, — so loving as a father, so kind as a friend, and so great as a philosopher.

"'My father!' said Eveline with emotion, 'are you displeased with me? I love him!'

"'My dear child,' said he with ineffable tenderness, 'it is for your happiness. How can I be displeased with you? Act as your own heart dictates.'

"Then, turning to me, he said: 'Vladimir, into your keeping I intrust my child. I know that you will make her happy. I am only grieved that you cannot remain here. There is no salvation for those politically outlawed in Russia. Nor is there any hope for those under suspicion. It is only a question of time when I shall be called away from you. When I am away, Vladimir, do not forget that in this hour I have given you the most precious jewel in my possession, my Eveline. Cherish her, and promise me that in the future you will leave politics alone for her sake. Give me your hand.'

"I gave him my hand, while tears blinded my vision and sobs shook my frame. Poor Eveline! she threw herself on her father's breast and wept.

"We stood thus for several minutes. Datleff held his hands over our heads as in benediction.

"Suddenly, heavy treads and the clink of spurs were heard in the hall. 'Children,' said Count Datleff, 'my time has come.' He had hardly finished, when the doors opened and an officer of rank appeared.

"He bowed. 'It is my painful duty, Count,' he said, 'to ask you to accompany me.'

"'Very well, Baron Larin; I am ready,' said Datleff.

"With a cry of despair Eveline threw herself on her father's neck. 'O my dear father! let me go with you. Baron, you are an old friend, take me along. We are both guilty; we will suffer together.'

"I could see a nervous twitching in the Baron's face.

"'Order your affairs, Count,' said he, in a whisper. 'The castle is surrounded. I cannot help there; but you might secure your valuables. The young folks can take them away; they will be unmolested.'

"'Then assist them to leave the country,' said the Count.

"'I will,' Larin replied, and gave the Count his hand.

"Turning to Eveline, he continued: 'Countess, this house will be searched by the *Commissair*. If no inconvenient papers are found, there might yet be hope.'

"'Impossible,' said the Count. 'There is enough evidence in this house of my free thoughts to send me to Siberia for life. Baron, I will go with you.'

"'They shall not find the evidence,' cried Eveline, and before we could stop her, she caught a firebrand from the hearth and ran into her father's study. Larin shook his head and smiled, but made no effort to follow her, and in a few minutes we saw the flames rise and the smoke fill the house. Not until the fire had made sufficient headway, did Larin open the door to the hall and give the alarm to the soldiers. But nothing could be done; and before the *Commissair* arrived, Badin Castle was in flames.

"'My duty is done,' whispered Larin as he saw the *Commissair;* 'you are saved, Count. I think the minister will revoke the order for your arrest now.'

"This was so; the *Commissair* telegraphed an 'utter lack of incriminating evidence,' after he and the Count had held a brief conversation.

"'I have paid dearly for our liberty,' said Datleff to us, a few hours later, while on our way to Moscow, 'but I am not deceived by the Minister's revocation. I repeat, it is but a question of time.'

"We were quietly married in Moscow, and prepared for our journey to Switzerland. On the afternoon of the third day after our arrival at Moscow, Count Datleff said: 'My children, I have concluded to go to Berlin, and have procured passports for Eveline and myself. You, Vladimir, will travel on your own passport. I consider it safer.'

" We rejoiced at this news, and the next morning found us comfortably lodged in our sleeping-car, on the train going to Berlin.

"I breathed more freely when I had passed the Russian frontier. We staid in Berlin six weeks, and were ready to proceed to Berne, in Switzerland. I had gone out to say good by to some friends. I might have been out a little more than an hour; but when I returned to the hotel, both Eveline and her father were gone.

"Believing them on a promenade, I took a book and read. But when, after two hours, they still remained away, I grew restless.

"I was just going down to inquire, when the porter came up and handed me a card.

"'Bear up, darling; we are taken to our doom.
"'Eveline.'

"'Who gave you this card?' I asked the porter, with a passion that made him stand back.

"'The young lady,' he said. 'Three men came here in a closed carriage, and the old gentleman and the young lady went with them.'

"I heard no more, nor did I see anything. I seemed to sink into black space. For weeks I hovered between life and death. I rallied for a brief time, and went to Switzerland; but I feel that my time has come.

"Adieu, my dear friend, till we meet in a happier life. Yours ever,

"Vladimir."

"Wonderful," said Anderson.

"Yes; the ways of the Russians are queer," Burton rejoined. "Here is a dispatch, evidently sent to Vladimir after his death." The dispatch ran as follows:—

"Count Datleff and his daughter have been pardoned and their possessions restored. They are on their way to Berne. Larin."

"This dispatch was sent to me with a lot of papers and the notice of Vladimir's death," remarked Burton.

"Poor fellow!" said Anderson.

THE AUTOMATIC EXECUTIONER.

"MR. GIERS, Feldon has gone, and left things down in Mexico in confusion. I have just received a dispatch; he has taken along all the stock, securities, and the private papers. You must go down at once and look the matter up. Get those papers at all hazards. As the scoundrel left but yesterday, he must be within reach. My private car will take you as far as the City of Mexico; there you take the narrow gauge to Orizaba. Your old friend Jackson will meet you at the station and assist you. Get ready. Steam is up; in five minutes you will have to start."

The morrow was to have been my wedding-day. I was sorry to think of the annoyance which this sudden departure would cause my beautiful Beatrice and her family. I had long learned to make the interests of my chief my own; delay was impossible; I could not even bid them good by. Duty before everything.

With feelings in which bitterness was curiously blended with satisfaction — satisfaction with the new evidence of confidence that I was giving — I said that I would be ready.

Returning to my office, I hastily wrote a note to Beatrice, took a box of cigars, and in another two minutes found myself in the chief's private car. He handed me written instructions and a check-book, and wishing me a safe journey, gave the signal to the engineer. A shrill whistle, and away we sped at a tremendous rate.

I read the instructions carefully. Special stress was laid upon the recovery of those private papers which the chief had mentioned. Being acquainted with the country, I was sanguine of success, if I could but get hold of Feldon, although I did not know him personally.

We reached El Paso almost before I knew it. On we sped through Mexico, until we arrived at Queretaro, where an accident happened to the car. Fortunately we were within twenty minutes of the night express from Aguas Calientes to the City of Mexico, which stops in Queretaro.

Having telegraphed to the chief regarding the accident, I ordered the car and the engine side-tracked until the next day, and procured a ticket for a first-class compartment to the City of Mexico.

I say "a first-class compartment" because the ticket agent had informed me that the express was made up of English coaches, with doors on both sides. I don't feel myself called upon to discuss the difference between English coaches and American cars, but although there are some disadvantages in English coaches, owing to the fact that the passengers face each other, a first-class compartment, when occupied by one or two passengers, is certainly far more convenient than the American car, with its two-seat chairs. The seats, which run the whole width of the English compartment-coaches, are comfortably upholstered, with soft arm-rests and head-cushions.

I was talking with the engineer, who swore at the Mexicans in choice machine-shop terms, when the express rushed into the station. I was ushered into a compartment by the conductor; the engine gave a shriek, and we sped toward the City of Mexico.

The light in the compartment being rather dim, I did not, on entering, observe the presence of any other person. But I was made aware that I had a fellow-traveler by something like a growl. My companion had evidently been disturbed in his slumber, and did not greatly relish it. As I looked more closely, I saw that he was well dressed, of gigantic size, and evidently an American. I apologized for the intrusion, but he made no answer. I had been traveling alone the whole day, and was inclined to talk to some one, so, nothing daunted, I stepped across to his corner, and offered him a cigar; he refused, and turned his head towards the window.

I said no more, and, drawing my soft felt over my eyes, I tried to sleep. But — how shall I say it? — a mysterious power seemed to keep me awake. Opening my eyes, they met the steady gaze of the stranger. Again

I closed them, and feigned sleep by a good imitation of a snore, while I looked at him through half-closed lids.

His gaze was still upon me; turn as I might, my eyes reverted to his, and the annoyance which I felt at first soon changed into horror, for suddenly his eyes took that strange brilliancy peculiar to savage beasts and the insane. The longer I looked at him, the firmer my conviction grew that I was the companion of a madman. It is literally true that this knowledge positively paralyzed me, for as I thought of rising, I could not move. The horror grew so intense that I felt the perspiration oozing from every pore of my body.

Thoughts chased one another through my brain with the rapidity of lightning; my school days, my life as a newsboy, my meeting with the chief, my first step to an honored position, my lovely affianced, my rise to the highest position in the gift of the chief, my race after Feldon,—all flashed before my mind; and there I was, my eyes spellbound by those of the madman.

I tried to recall my energy; I sought to coax my limbs into mobility. I reasoned with my fingers, asking them to move just a little; I knew if they but moved one hundredth of an inch, I should be safe. I tried to persuade them to move in the direction of my overcoat pocket, where I had my revolver. Life is so sweet (I reasoned); I am young, beloved, and well to do, and you know that I am a dead shot; move, oh, move just a little! All in vain; they could not or would not obey my will. In sheer despair I tried to scream, but while I heard the wheels roll upon the rails, heard the breathing of the madman, whose face was livid with mania, and heard the beating of my own heart, I could not utter a sound. My God! Dumb and palsied in the bloom of life, in the chase after fortune, at the gate of domestic paradise! Help! help! But no sound escaped my lips, and those terrible eyes still upon me!

Now he rose and slowly came to my side. What a tremendous fellow he was! — his head touched the ceiling. He stooped and looked into my eyes; his glance went right through me. He put his hand into my overcoat pocket, out of which he took my revolver and slipped it into his own pocket; as he did so he smiled a ghastly smile, more horrifying even than his gaze. Now he tapped me on the forehead, at the same time saying, "Get up, Mister!"

His touch acted on me like a powerful battery; I was up in an instant. Strange to say, and as I stood on my feet, my faculties returned, but with them the recognition that I was absolutely at the disposition of the merciless maniac.

For a moment I thought he had hypnotized me, and wanted some sport, but I soon found out my mistake; he was obviously insane.

"What do you want of me, sir?" I cried.

"I want *you!*" he replied, ferociously.

"You want my money, I suppose. Here it is," and I handed him my pocket-book.

"Keep your money; I am not a robber; I am a philanthropist."

"And what do you want of me?"

"I want to show you an invention of my own; the automatic executioner."

"I shall be pleased to see it," said I.

"Shall you? I am glad of that."

With this he took from his pocket a curiously twisted cord, and continued thus: "I have worked on this for years, and am at last ready to show the world what real genius is like. As sheriff of Montreal, I have executed many criminals in my time, but their last struggle was always a disgusting sight. My invention does away with all this; one end of the electro-automatic executioner is fastened to a hook, the noose is slipped over the criminal's head, and in a fraction of a second he is with the silent majority. Do you see the advantage of my invention?"

I thought it advisable to humor the trend of his mania, and said, "This is truly a great invention. I should like to introduce this among the politicians of San Francisco."

"Introduce it, eh? Why, yes, certainly; it shall be introduced, but I will do that myself!"

"And what do you want me to do in the matter?" I asked, trembling as the thought dawned upon me that he possibly wanted to try his invention on me. His answer confirmed my fears. He said:

"You? Why, you shall be made glorious by verifying the utility of my invention. I have been hunting in every country in the world for the proper person, worthy enough for that grand purpose, but Heaven bade me wait until this evening. I knew you would come, and am prepared to execute Heaven's command."

Imagine my horror! If I could have fainted, I should have experienced relief, and would have been executed without consciousness. But my nerves had grown strong during the last moments. I had perfect control over my faculties and feelings, and thought of means to escape an untimely death.

Involuntarily I looked at the bell-cord line, which, unfortunately for me, was on the other side of the compartment.

Madmen are cunning; he caught my look, and said, "It is useless to look for that rope there; this train does not stop at any of the way-stations; nor would Heaven permit this work to be interrupted. When we reach the City of Mexico, I shall be famous and you in heaven!"

For a moment I thought of jumping at the door, opening it, and saving myself; but the idea was not feasible, because, at the rate the train was moving, I would be dashed to death, were I lucky enough to escape the grasp of the powerful maniac.

"Make haste," said he, drawing his watch; "the execution must be completed before five, and it is now twenty minutes to five."

This intelligence caused me a thrill of joy; since force would only hasten my awful end, I must seek to gain time. The train was due in the City of Mexico at five o'clock; if I could divert him for that length of time, I was saved.

"My dear sir," said I, "I am quite willing that you should try your invention on me, but before I die, I ask you to grant me a favor."

"What is it? Speak! it is granted."

"I wish to write my will, and a letter to a lady to whom I am betrothed, and would ask you to mail the letters in the City of Mexico. Will you do that?"

"Certainly, with pleasure; only be quick about it."

"I thank you very much. Ah, how provoking!" said I, searching in my pockets. "I have no paper to write the letters. Could you oblige me with a sheet of paper?"

"Certainly, sir; I have plenty of that," said he, extracting from his breast-pocket a tablet of paper and two envelopes.

While he was taking the paper from his pocket, I managed to break the point of my pencil.

"Just see how troublesome I am! The point of my pencil has broken off, and I have no knife to sharpen it."

"Oh, no trouble at all," he replied. "Just hand me the pencil and I will sharpen it for you." With this he took a keen-edged dagger from the belt under his coat and sharpened the pencil. He was evidently as well armed as he was physically powerful. Having sharpened the pencil, he sheathed his dagger, and told me to go on.

I thought of writing a lot of nonsense, but could not, for the life of me, — which really was at stake, — compose a simple sentence. In my despair I copied the alphabet. I drew the characters with care, in order to fill up time and space. Oh, my sorry fate! how slowly the moments passed by! how miserably slow the train moved on! I had often whistled a-gallop to the "tac" the wheels were beating as they touched the connecting points of the rail, but now they were so slow that funeral music would have required a quicker *tempo*.

At last the sheet was full, and my executioner asked me if I were ready.

"I am ready with my will, but I have not written the letter to my affianced."

"Well, write quickly," said he, and his look was threatening.

"I should like to describe to her your wonderful invention. Can you show me how it works, so that I may write intelligently on the subject."

"Decidedly, I will. You are a good fellow, entirely unlike those cowards in Montreal."

"Ah, but where will you fasten it?" I asked.

"Nothing easier; I slip the end through that lamp-bracket in the ceiling,—just the place for it."

So said, so done; but while he was thus occupied, I cast a glance at the window, and my heart gave a leap, for I saw the first houses of the great Mexican city. To gain a little more time was all that I needed; but my life depended on my doing so.

"Behold how it is done," said he, holding the cord in one hand.

"Ah, but you would have to engage a living executioner to slip the noose over the criminal's head," I argued.

"There is where you are at fault. You need no one at all to assist in the execution. The criminal himself slips it over his head, the automatic executioner being so charged with electricity that it no sooner touches his neck than it kills him."

He became frightfully excited, and in his rage did not hear the whistle of the locomotive. The sound inspired me with hope and courage. Now, another minute and I am safe!

"This is indeed the greatest invention of the age," said I.

"The only thing that perplexes me is how you prevent the criminal from slipping out of the noose. You would then need a man, after all, to keep the noose in the proper place."

"There is the great point of my invention. The electricity draws the noose together the instant it slips over his head and—"

"Can you draw?" I interrupted him.

"No," he replied. "Why?"

"Because, I should like to send my affianced a sketch of this wonderful executioner; she would enjoy it. But as you cannot draw, and as I, who am a first-class sketcher, could not possibly make a sketch after my death, she will have to do without it. She will be doubly sorry, because she edits a newspaper.

"A newspaper, did you say?" he cried, his eyes flashing wildly. "They refused to mention my invention in the papers in Montreal, the curs!"

"My affianced would be only be too happy to do it, if —"

"If what?" he cried. "Why don't you finish?"

"I was going to say, if you would consent to slip the noose over your head, so that I might sketch you. She would publish the description only if it is accompanied by a sketch."

"This is a capital idea," said he; "and if you are quick about it, I'll do it."

"I will be quick," I cried. "Get ready."

I had hardly finished when he slipped the cord over his head; but quicker than thought I was at the door, opened it, and jumped. I fell into a crowd of people,—we were at the station of the City of Mexico. As I jumped I heard the gurgling sounds of the strangling maniac. Regaining my feet I hastened to the compartment, anticipating the horrible sight of the madman, strangled by the invention of his disordered mind. But imagine my surprise, when, on reaching the place of my late adventure, I found it — vacant.

Had I been dreaming, or was I mad? Had all that I suffered been an hallucination?

The curious crowd made such a noise that the conductor came forward, eager to know the cause of the tumult. I asked him if he knew my traveling companion,— if he had seen him leave. He looked at me in blank astonishment; he had seen no one leave the compartment except myself, —in the peculiar manner described. He said that I had been the sole occupant of that compartment from Queretaro; and, turning to the crowd, said, in Spanish, "The American is crazy." This caused the crowd to disperse, panic-stricken. Seeing that I could get no satisfactory explanation from the conductor, I took my overcoat and bought a ticket for Orizaba. At the station there I was met by Jackson, who received me very cordially, and informed me that Feldon had been found. I had experienced so many shocks in the last few hours, that this news hardly surprised me. Still, I asked, "Where was he found?"

"In Jalapa," was Jackson's reply.

"When was that?" I queried.

"Last night," said Jackson.

"What has he got to say?" said I, sternly.

"To say!" cried Jackson; "the poor fellow has nothing to say; he is as crazy as a loon. I pity him. It took six men to manage him last night."

We had just arrived at the quartz-mills, and Jackson conducted me into the room where Feldon was strapped to an iron bedstead, a raving maniac. As I looked into his face, I nearly fell, the shock was so tremendous. Great God! it was my traveling companion of the night before!

When I told Jackson the cause of my agitation, he was perplexed. "The automatic executioner is the very thing he raved about. We found him half dead, with a riata around his neck. This is very strange!" said Jackson.

My story met with many incredulous smiles in San Francisco. My dear wife alone believes it. "It is the projected consciousness, or your *Astral Body*, that experienced all this," she says.

A SACRIFICE TO SCIENCE.

I.

THERE are many people living now, who will recall with a shudder the frightful epidemic which raged in the city of San Francisco a score of years ago. This epidemic was a malignant typhoid fever, which made its appearance first in the hospital of the county jail. More than fifty-eight convicts died in one summer of that mysterious disease, which manifested always the same symptoms and always ended with a fatal result. The people in the city knew at first very little of this dreadful calamity; moreover, they were quite unconcerned whether more or fewer convicts lived or died behind the massive walls of the county's penal institute. However, the newspapers soon spread the matter abroad; people became cognizant of the danger that threatened the community. Thus far, the people of San Francisco had been mercifully spared; but while some spoke in whispers about the epidemic which was raging among the outcasts of society, others spoke with pride of Dr. Clinton, the penitentiary physician, who had discovered the disease, and was the first to give a minute description of it. He had not been able to cure any of the convicts, but his fame had reached the remotest corners of the civilized world.

Dr. Clinton lived in a gloomy house at the outer end of Broadway, which stood alone in a block of land. He was not very sociable, but that did not prevent the wealthiest people from calling him to their houses.

Dr. Clinton was born in the city of New York, had graduated from the medical college at quite an early age, had gone to Europe, and after years and years of hard study at the great universities, had at last gone with a scientific expedition to study the fever epidemic and other noxious diseases among the natives of the West Indies, finally settling in San Francisco.

Some of the younger physicians were enthusiastic about Dr. Clinton's discovery (the older practitioners were less demonstrative), and adored his fine scholarship. It was a pity, they said, that he was so exclusive, and buried himself in the old house on Broadway, when society was eager to lionize him. The Doctor paid no attention to gossip, either favorable or otherwise. The prison and his gloomy house on Broadway were his world; he was satisfied.

With Dr. Clinton lived his sister, Alvira,

who kept house for him, and a dismal-looking servant by the name of Mort, who had accompanied the doctor on his travels.

Alvira Clinton was wealthy in her own right; her parents, at their death, had left her and her brother enough means to live in luxury all their lives, but the Doctor's love of science had made him careless of ease.

Alvira Clinton, without being very beautiful, lacked by no means a certain attractiveness. She had big black eyes, which were expressive of intelligence; about her mouth there was that peculiar expression said to be expressive of an indomitable will. But when Alvira talked she was positively handsome. There was a bubbling over of spirit, a sparkling of wit, that charmed all men. She talked but seldom now; her devotion to her brother, her tireless help in his scientific labors, occupied her time. She did not care for society, its gossip and its parties, but was seen more frequently in the houses of the poor, her neighbors and well-wishers. She went to see them because, curiously enough, the miserable Mexicans in the neighborhood were afraid to enter the gloomy house, which was surrounded by a high fence and tall eucalyptus trees.

At a short distance from the house was a large stable containing the animals on which the Doctor experimented, and which Mort called the "Clinic."

Alvira shuddered when she heard her brother give the details for the dog clinic; the whinings of the tortured animals filled her with unspeakable horror. This annoyed her brother, and he made her enter the gruesome hospital. He desired her to satisfy herself that the animals were not being tortured, and that the noise came from the dogs playing in the garden. Alvira was compelled to acknowledge that the animals in the "Clinic" were quite as lively as the dogs in the garden; there was no sign of cruelty, nor even harshness, visible; everything was kept scrupulously clean, making quite a pleasing impression. Of course, there were several of the sick rabbits stretched out in their cages; the light had gone from their eyes, and they seemed to wait for the end which was sure to come. But this had to be; it was in perfect harmony with a hospital.

"Are you satisfied now?" Dr. Clinton asked his sister.

"Yes," said Alvira; "still, I think I had better keep away from your clinic."

"Suit yourself," said he, calmly. It was just as well she staid away; he had no need of her there, and she might be in Mort's way. The latter attended to all the business in that domain.

Mort was Clinton's right-hand man. He was absolutely indispensable. He contrived to keep the "Clinic" supplied with the animals necessary for anatomical purposes and to dispose of them after that. Alvira hated him because he seemed too familiar with her brother. She shuddered when he came near her; he was so repulsive-looking. From the back of his head to his forehead there was not a hair. His head looked like a huge ball of polished ivory. He had neither brows nor eyelashes, and his nose was flattened down to a wide mouth with colorless lips and immense teeth. His body was lank and his clothes too wide. The skin of his face and hands looked like yellow parchment drawn taut. One invariably imagined that his clothes covered a horrible skeleton. And this individual, at the sight of whom dogs drew in their tails and ran away, had the fullest confidence of her brother.

"No one outside of the Doctor and myself shall see what we are about in our hospital," he once said to a presumptuous reporter. And thus they lived, secluded from the world, with nothing to disturb them. The many famous physicians and the lesser lights who had come to study the peculiar disease, and had expected to be treated hospitably by Dr. Clinton, were somewhat disappointed. Not that he did not treat them with the necessary civility, but while he took them to the prison hospital, he coldly refused to admit them to his private study or to Mort's "Clinic." They should neither see his notes nor the means he employed to check the disease.

His persistent refusal to show his private "workshop" caused the learned doctors to shake their heads suspiciously. Clinton saw it and bit his lips; but when they had gone his rage was uncontrollable. "The idiots!" he cried, and ran into the garden, racing up and down. Mort, who knew the cause of the Doctor's rage, roundly abused the "Eastern quacks." This invariably had a pacifying effect upon the Doctor. He smiled, and a defiant look came into his face. Let them shake their heads. Mort and himself, and not a living human soul besides, should enter his sanctum until the work is done.

Any person who ventured into the garden or into the house was treated most ungraciously by Mort. "What do you want? We don't receive visitors," was the stereotyped remark with which he sent away men and women.

However, one man, George Dalton, was an exception. He alone dared to enter the lonely house without being sent away.

II.

George Dalton was a lawyer who had known the Clinton family in New York, and had transacted their business there. He had asked Mr. Alfred Clinton, Sen., for permission to pay his respects to the only daughter, but was met with such harshness by the old gentleman that he did not make a second attempt. Of course, George Dalton was an impecunious young lawyer, but he was young, well educated, of a jovial disposition, and quite hopeful. When the old Mr. Clinton told Dalton that he could aspire to transact the legal business of the family, and to nothing else, George said nothing. But he no sooner left the Clinton mansion than he proceeded to the nearest barber, had his blonde locks and beard cut and shaved, went home, packed his portmanteau, and went West. In less than five years George Dalton had made a reputation and a fortune; but his early timidity never left him. He recalled the words of Clinton, Sen., and he staid in the city of San Francisco.

Ten years more had gone by and one day George saw Alvira on the street. The hot wave that suffused his face when he saw her clearly told that years and space had no effect upon his affections. Alvira, too, was happy to see him. She told him of the death of her parents, of her brother's great learning and fame, and their intention to locate in the city. They were indeed a handsome pair as they walked up Broadway. Dr. Clinton was favorable to Dalton, as far as he was capable of showing his regard. He spoke a word or two with the friend of his sister, and then left them alone. Dr. Clinton had no interest in anything or anybody that did not betray the symptoms of typhoid fever. But when George Dalton succeeded in getting him the position in the prison hospital, he condescended to express his appreciation, not to Dalton, but to Alvira. She was happy that he thought well of George; for, be it understood, she loved the lawyer, and would have followed him, were it not that she pitied her brother, who would have been helpless without her. Nor could she think of leaving him alone with his "evil genius," as she called Mort.

Dr. Clinton was sure of his sister. He knew that she would not leave him for any man. He did not object to Dalton's visits, which, however, were not so frequent as to cause him any uneasiness. Every Sunday evening the gloomy house, or, to be more precise, the family sitting-room, was enlivened by George Dalton's pleasant conversation; and because Alvira seemed to enjoy the lively chit-chat, her brother rather encouraged the visitor. Without it, the Doctor thought she might tire of the loneliness and gloom, and — who knows? — might leave him alone — the very thought caused him to shudder — with his factotum, Mort. The latter knew that this thought upset the Doctor, and he never failed to allude to it. These allusions enraged Clinton, and he would have chastised his servant or dismissed him — if he could. But as he could not do either, he raved in impotent rage, and then consoled himself with the thought that Alvira was too sensible to entertain any such ideas. How could she?

One bright, sunny morning, it was on a Sunday, a scene was enacted in Dr. Clinton's garden that caused Alvira to weep, the Doctor to rave, and Mort to grin; and when Mort grinned, the birds in the trees ceased their chirping and flew away; everything seemed to wither when Mort's eyes glistened and Mort's mouth grinned. The scene was as follows: In an altana in the garden sat George Dalton, Alvira, and the Doctor. Dalton seemed depressed, — strange for a man of his temper; the Doctor was smoking, and Alvira was speaking rather hastily and incoherently. At some distance, but near enough for him to hear, was Mort with his dogs. Clinton had just thrown away the stump of a cigar, and Alvira, glad at the pretext, went into the house to fetch some fresh cigars.

Dalton took advantage of Alvira's absence and said, "I might as well say it now as at any other time. Dr. Clinton, I love Almira; have loved her for years, and have reason to believe that she is not indifferent to me. In a word, I desire to marry your sister. She shall never have any cause to regret it. Give us your consent, Doctor."

Dr. Clinton seemed to think of a proper expression to couch his refusal. Dalton's speech had evidently displeased him, but it did not come unexpected. He had grown tired of the lawyer's visits. He wanted absolute seclusion. If the lawyer suffered a second rebuff, he was sure to stay away for good. He stroked his beard, and a smile of satisfaction flitted across his pale face.

"You are speaking of an impossibility, Dalton," he said. "My sister has concluded, once for all, to devote her life to such an unworthy old bachelor as I am."

But you cannot — you dare not — accept such a sacrifice, Dr. Clinton," said Dalton. "Alvira is not the girl to spend her life in the society of that fellow Mort and his dogs. You ought to be more reasonable, Doctor."

Dr. Clinton rose from his seat. He was a shade paler than usual. His dark eyes shot flashes of malignant hatred and contempt. Dalton involuntarily stepped back as the Doctor hissed the answer into his face: "Whether I have the right to accept the sacrifice of my sister,— if to resign the drudgery of a commonplace marriage can be called a sacrifice,— this, I judge, is no business of a stranger."

"But I am—"

"A stranger for us," said the Doctor. "You could have spared yourself this explanation if your feelings had been less youthful than your age would lead one to believe."

George Dalton was astounded, but he gradually gained his balance. "We two are done, Dr. Clinton," he said. "Miss Alvira is of age, and mistress of her own action. I will ask her to decide."

"There she is," said Clinton. " I will leave you two alone, so that you do not accuse me of influencing her decision."

When Alvira returned she was astonished to find her brother and Dalton facing each other in evident excitement. Clinton cut the matter short by saying: "Alvira, Mr. Dalton desires to speak to you. I will, in the mean time, look after Mort's boarders."

Alvira took a seat and motioned Dalton to do likewise. But when Dalton was about to speak, she said, "Do not speak." Her voice was soft and sad. " Whatever changes you desire to bring about, do not count upon my consent. Years ago, yes; but now it is different. I feel it is my sacred duty to care for Alfred, who would be lost without me. Besides, I do not feel at all lonely," she added, with all the feminine tenderness she was capable of, "since you come to the house. Leave matters as they are. We have peace; do not disturb the mutual harmony."

"My dear Alvira, what you have said," replied Dalton, "demonstrates to me one fact, namely, that you appreciate my visits, and because of that I tell you, if you do love me a little, you will not refuse me. You will not cast aside the true devotion of a man tried and found loyal. I say again, Alvira, be my wife."

The girl looked at Dalton with eyes that mirrored the gratitude of her soul. She knew that she loved him, and had he taken her to his breast in youthful passion, she would have followed him. She would have forsaken her brother, if Dalton had kissed the confession from her lips. But as he appeared in a matter of fact manner, speaking friendly and sensibly, it was her duty to be sensible, too, and this demanded that she tell him where her duty lay, namely, with her brother. The reason why she would not leave him was that he was sacrificing his health and his life to science. She said it with a sigh that clearly told of her sufferings.

"Then you stay with him out of sheer pity?" Dalton asked.

Alvira took hold of Dalton's hand, and with every evidence of anxiety she said: "Forgive me, George, but I cannot act otherwise. My brother believes in my faithful love and devotion, and he shall not be disappointed. On the day that he needs my life it shall be fettered by no other bonds. I must be at his side."

Alvira sank back into her seat and covered her face with her hands. Dalton saw the tears trickle through her fingers. His heart ached to see the woman he loved suffer so much.

"Your brother is ill. He ought to give up his work. Let him travel,—anything that will keep him away from his labors," said he.

"You are right," said Alvira. "His work will be his death; but he cannot live without it. You ought to have seen him when he discovered the first case at the prison hospital. He had evidently been baffled by something in his investigations, and the epidemic at the hospital had come at the most opportune moment. He suffered, nevertheless, because he believed himself responsible for every person that died, —as if he, and not God, had brought on the epidemic. The first evening — when the dread disease made its appearance — was the most horrible. I shall never forget it. He came into the house without saying a word, and ran out into the garden again, running up and down as if possessed, trampling upon flowers and the shrubbery, and laughing loudly. It terrified me, but I did not dare to speak to him. He is quiet now, and with nothing to excite him, we live quite happily. And now I see the dark clouds again. This time, dear friend, you are the disturber. For my sake, George, be friends with Alfred, and when you come again do not broach that other subject."

"My dear Miss Alvira, I am grieved to tell you that after the hard words that have passed between your brother and me it would be quite impossible for me to call at his house again; but granted I did come, it would be equally impossible for me to subdue my feelings, now more than ever, since I know how unhappy you are."

He rose and stretched out his hand, which she grasped, saying: "I know that you will forever remain my dearest, my best, friend, and because of that I ask you to promise me when I call you that you will come to me. Promise me, George!" He knew what she suffered, and without a word he pressed her hand in token of a promise, and left. Dr. Clinton saw Dalton, the only friend of the family, leave the house, but he seemed to be engrossed in some subject which Mort had shown him, and did not turn.

III.

Added to gossip that Dalton's withdrawal occasioned, was the fact that the Doctor's star was on the wane. The people became disappointed in Dr. Clinton. It is true, he had made a great discovery, and the medical journals all over the world were still discussing the subject; but suffering and death are old evils, and the discovery of one more disease was interesting, but not quite agreeable to contemplate, considering that one might become a victim to the new discovery. Dr. Clinton had not found a remedy against the epidemic, and therefore had achieved nothing.

But this was not all. He had managed to make more enemies than any man in his profession. When he had become the fashion in the city, and every one consulted the eminent "fever doctor," he was found deficient in that one quality, — a *sine qua non* to the success of a physician, — to flatter the rich, to humor their ills, especially the female patients, and be interested in the babies of fond mothers. To make matters worse, it so happened that he had some differences with one of the prison directors, who told him that he (Dr. Clinton) was merely an official at the hospital, but not the master. And last, but not least for Dr. Clinton, was the fact that the epidemic had disappeared as suddenly as it had come.

People began to lose their dread of the disease and their respect for the discoverer. Added to this was the opinion of a prominent college professor of New York, who had spent months in the city to investigate the disease. "This disease is not a new discovery," the professor said, "and it is due to the boundless conceit of Dr. Clinton that it was given so much prominence. If Dr. Clinton had discovered a mode by which the organic disease germs can be developed and scientifically explained, if he have found the bacillus and learned to conquer its poisonous and deadly effect, let him proclaim it, and the world would hail him a Messiah. If he had not done this, he had not merited any recognition, outside of the fact that he had opened one more of the many problems which science is working hard to solve. However, the problem was not put by Dr. Clinton, but by his suffering patients. Dr. Clinton," the professor concluded, " has done nothing; he has not even attempted to save the lives of those who fell victims to the fever."

The opinion of this eminent man, being published, had the effect that not one person could be found in the city of San Francisco who would consent to be treated by Dr. Clinton. Even the poorest people were afraid to consult him, and only those who could not get the services of any other physician free of charge called him to their bedsides.

But that peculiarly malignant smile never left Dr. Clinton's lips. In the fever ward of the prison hospital he was still master; there no one interfered with him.

But one day the whole matter came to a sudden end. Dr. Clinton came home and told Alvira that he had been dismissed. Alvira desired to know what cause the Directors had for such an action.

"They at first made all sorts of charges," said Clinton. "I was too independent. I told them I would consult them in the future on all matters. Then they trumped up a charge of infidelity. One of them — the fellow is a deacon in a church — objected to an atheistic physician; and that cur pretends to be an American. I laughed in their faces at first, but ultimately promised that for the sake of peace I would go to church and partake of communion, or that I would embrace any faith they pleased."

"You would not have done that," said Alvira. "I don't believe it! You would never have sacrificed your honor; because to dissemble is dishonorable."

Clinton looked at his sister with a contemptuous smile upon his lips.

"I have laid so many sacrifices upon the altar of science and investigation," said he, grimly, "that a lie more or less could not possibly make much difference. But they would not consider my proposition.

"The next charge was, that I was too extravagant at the cost of the institution, by giving chickens and wine to the prisoners. Poor devils! I should have deprived them of the necessary nutriment, while I am experimenting on their carcasses. To hamper my work on account of such trifles! I mastered myself, and promised to let the sick starve as much as possible. But it came out at last. They told me that I do not prescribe any medicine for the sick. Not prescribe enough medicine! Ha, ha, ha!

"After this I was, of course, forced to leave. The professional honor demanded that I should leave! The professional honor! Ha, ha, ha! Do these fools think I am like those quacks who believe, and make their patients believe, that they can and will cure them? We are not here for the sake of hospitals, but hospitals are here for our sakes, — for the sake of science. But there was no use fighting; they had made up their minds to get rid of me, and I went."

His restless eyes gazed upon the instruments in the cabinet, then upon the big volumes in his library. There, upon long shelves, stood a fine selection of all the classical and standard medical works from Aristotle down to Pasteur. Alvira understood his looks. Among these princes of science, among the greatest of the great, should be Dr. Clinton's work on the origin and cause of fever germs and their conquest. Otherwise he had nothing to live for. Alvira, with the instinct of a tender woman, found the right words to encourage her brother. "You are on the road to fame already; in fact, you are near the goal, and in spite of the petty jealousy of small men, you will yet be glorious, brother. You have made all the observations at the hospital that you needed, and as the epidemic is on the wane, it would be the proper time to bring your work to a close." Clinton seemed absent-minded, but at Alvira's last words he shook his head, and said, as if speaking to himself: "But three months more and I would have been done. I could have offered to the world the very greatest work of science, — a collection of deadly and of protecting bacilli."

But Alvira staid by her argument. "Of course, I am not competent to judge," she said; "but from the information which I gleaned from your remarks made at odd moments, I am inclined to think that new cases of the dread disease could hardly make much difference, and should the epidemic break out again at the hospital, I am sure they will have to call you. Who else could fill your place?"

"The epidemic is gone. I was mistaken. It does not make its appearance where bunglers are at work," Clinton said with a hoarse laugh, while his right hand mechanically played with his golden hypodermic injector. He then took up a book and was soon engrossed in his reading. His sister took it as a good omen. "He may yet succeed, and be counted among the foremost men of all times," she said, going to her own room.

But Alvira's hopes were not fulfilled. He grew darker and moodier every day. He lost all interest in his dog clinic, and when Mort approached to make some report regarding one of the animals he drove him away.

"Go to the devil with your dog stories," Alvira heard her brother scream at the top of his voice. "I do not need dogs. I need human beings, and these were taken from me, — stolen. Not even a condemned murderer would they give me."

Alvira could not hear Mort's answer, but she heard his tuneless laughter and a cry of rage from her brother, who threatened to knock him down.

IV.

Not like a young physician anxious for practice, but like a panting deer crying for water, did Dr. Clinton look for a patient. A patient! — only one sick person whom he could study; but he looked in vain. Not a soul came to the house. Alvira went from room to room and sighed. She never left the house now, and Mort, who attended to all affairs on the outside, came and went like a shadow. No one in the vicinity or in any part of the city thought of calling Dr. Clinton.

Unable to bear it any longer, the Doctor left the house, incognito, to find a patient, if possible. He entered the huts of the poorest people and bribed them with food and wine. He gave the parents money and the children candy, until he had gained their confidence. Then he told them that he was a physician, and when any one complained he volunteered his services. His life received a fresh impetus; he was happy. His science had found new material for investigation; Dr. Clinton was himself once more.

The best reason for his good humor was not so much the new and varied practice which he had found as the fact that the fever had made its appearance among the Mexicans in lower Broadway. It was as yet in its mildest form, but it was there, evidently and unmistakably. That no cases were reported from the prison hospital was probably due to the ignorance of the physicians, Dr. Clinton said. Those bunglers would not know the disease if they were laid low with it themselves. There was but one Dr. Clinton !

As the months passed, it was noticed that the epidemic had reached a very dangerous degree. None had died as yet; the Doctor's art had conquered death thus far, but the epidemic raged with frightful violence.

It was in the spring of the year that the poor people whom Dr. Clinton had assisted with food, medicine, and money grew to suspect a compact between Dr. Clinton and the Devil. This suspicion was fostered by the relentless hatred of an old Mexican fisherman whom the Doctor had had the misfortune to displease. As the old Mexican was the oracle among his kind, his words carried weight. "He is in league with the Devil," he was heard to say. "Look out for yourselves; he brings you the sickness." But there were some who laughed at the padre, and told him to consult the Doctor for the affection of the eyes. After much persuasion the old Mexican so far mastered his antagonism as to send for Dr. Clinton. The latter performed an operation with so much skill and success that the populace danced with joy, and told the old padre that he was mistaken about the good Doctor. Nothing could now have shaken their faith in Dr. Clinton, were it not that the old Mexican caught the fever. In his delirium he uttered frightful imprecations against the Doctor. When Clinton made his visit the next morning, he was met by a mob, who warned him to keep away from their houses, else he would get hurt. He tried to reason with them. He begged; he pleaded, — all in vain. "You are the Devil," they said. "You gave us food and money, and you bought us body and soul; but you shall not come here again. Wherever you go, there is death." And he was forced to retreat.

"The dogs! the curs!" he cried, running up and down in his study. "They are afraid of their miserable lives, as if their lives were worth anything, if they did not serve to enrich science. They want to live. Well, let them live, and starve."

As it was, these wretches had added their mite toward assisting his studies. The raging fever had revealed to him many new points of interest. If he could have brought one of those cases under the microscope, and if he could also have succeeded in curing a most violent case, his ambition would have been satisfied, his work done, and he would have laughed at their ingratitude. He was so excited that he discussed the subjects of his research with his sister and Mort. The latter taunted the Doctor with cowardice, to retreat before a mob of dirty Mexicans. Alvira suffered unspeakably. Why was her learned brother so haughty to everybody and so submissive to the taunts and insults of his servant? Did Mort know the *modus operandi* of the new method? and did her brother fear that his servant might reveal it to one of the many jealous physicians, who would benefit by the labors of her brother? Probably.

A few days later, Alvira and her brother were walking in the garden, arm in arm. Mort was busy tending to some plants, but his sharp ears never lost one word of the conversation between brother and sister.

"Ah! if I could only get to work again,—

to work among people, and not among rabbits and dogs in that clinic over there," said Clinton.

"Are you sure, Alfred," said Alvira, "that mankind will be benefited by your discovery?"

A contemptuous smile played about Mort's lips. Alvira caught that smile, and shivered.

"Mankind is but a drop in the ocean of nature," said Dr. Clinton, "and nature refuses to be helped. She laughs and jeers at us when we are presumptuous enough to attempt to conquer her. Nature is without consideration. She is the most powerful murderess in existence, and science, in order to know nature, must be in sympathy with her."

"But where is the benefit to mankind?" said Alvira, sick at heart.

"Our science, my dear Alvira," said

Clinton, with a smile, "knows of cases where enthusiastic pupils took poison to assist their perplexed masters in demonstrating its effects. You have heard of the painter's daughter who permitted herself to be crucified, so that her father might catch the proper expression for a picture of the Saviour? Natural science knows of such models who have sacrificed their lives mundane to live eternally in the sacred history of science. We live for science, not for mankind. Mort," the Doctor cried, "what do you say to the idea of advertising for such volunteers for scientific research?"

Clinton's eyes sparkled with a brilliancy and wildness that frightened his poor sister. Mort, however, seemed to have considered the Doctor's proposition. "We might try it," he said. "But I don't believe it would be a success. You cannot rely upon volunteers. One must take his subjects wherever he finds them."

Alvira was horrified to hear Mort speak so to her brother. In the mouth of the latter those words seemed but the exaggeration of an exuberant fancy, but in the mouth of Mort they sounded like the words of a scoundrel. She was so overcome that she could hardly stand. She ran into the house, that her brother might not notice her weakness.

For days after this conversation, Alvira shivered at the recollection, and remained in her room so as to avoid meeting her brother's evil genius.

Dr. Clinton's endeavors to visit the poor were met with determined opposition. When he showed himself, a shower of stones and other missiles met his advance; once he was even shot at. Had he incurred the displeasure of the Americans in the same degree as that of the superstitious Mexicans, he would have been tarred and feathered, if not shot. But when the Americans heard one of those absurd stories about the luckless Dr. Clinton, they merely laughed at the horror that was expressed in the faces of the " Greasers " at the mention of his name. They had wisely or providentially been spared an intimate acquaintance with Dr. Clinton's philanthropy.

But the repeated rebuffs that he suffered from the Mexicans doubled his energy and his desire for investigation. He experimented on the animals, and very soon all the dogs and rabbits in Mort's clinic lay either sick or dead. Mort pleaded in vain against the total extermination of his animals; he refused to bring new specimens, in spite of his master's commands and threats. A gruesome stillness had now fallen upon the lonely house and in the garden. Bruno, the big St. Bernard dog, was the sole animal left; he was Alvira's pet, and sacred. He greeted his master with mighty jumps, and gave a joyous howl whenever his mistress showed herself in the garden.

One bright morning, in the middle of May, as Mort entered the library, he found the dog lying on the floor, with red eyes, and its swollen tongue protruding from its mouth,— the dog had caught the fever. Mort uttered a hoarse laugh as he dragged the splendid animal into his "Clinic." Alvira was very sad when she heard of Bruno's illness, but she did not give up the hope of his recovery. The dog had been her brother's pet, and he would surely cure him.

As often as Dr. Clinton came from the "Clinic," she asked him after the dog's health. On the third day after Bruno's illness, Alvira concluded to see the poor animal herself, and, mastering her dislike for Mort and his establishment, the girl crossed the garden toward the "Clinic." But she halted at the door, because of the angry words which her brother spoke to Mort. The two were evidently engaged in a violent quarrel. The door was partly open, and Alvira could look into the experimental room without being seen. Dr. Clinton walked up and down, gesticulating wildly and uttering curses at his factotum, while the latter busied himself with cleansing the microscope, but kept a vigilant eye on his master.

"Your spite and obstinacy be damned!" cried the Doctor. "You miserable wretch, you would prevent me from completing my work by refusing to bring me the necessary subjects, eh? I have asked you again and again to bring some, but you have not brought me a mouse, even. I would like to experiment day and night, but am hampered by your obstinacy."

"Ha, ha, ha!" laughed Mort. This laugh caused Alvira's heart to stop. How dared the wretch be so insolent to her brother! She listened again.

"You are experimenting! Ha, ha, ha! Well, I don't propose to go to the penitentiary for stealing dogs. If I am to hang, I want to be as great as you are, Doctor. I shall then have done my share of work by the million."

"Shut up!" cried Dr. Clinton, his voice hoarse with passion. "You miserable cur, you know very well why I desire to complete my work just now. It is the last moment. I am maddened by the thought that while I am longing for subjects to finish my work some one else might publish a book on the subject, and spoil the work of a lifetime."

"No one in America or Europe can do that," replied Mort, with a grin. "To do what we have done one must have a steady hand like you, and be without prejudice. I can rely upon you! No one else could possibly accomplish your work. After Bruno's death there is nothing left but to experiment on yourself; who else would—"

"Shut up, or—" Alvira was unable to listen any longer; the knowledge that her brother had sacrificed his pet dog was too much for her. She understood that science could not have benefited by Bruno's death; that her brother must certainly have acted under mental stress. In that case, however, he was not bad; he was only unfortunate; his work and anxiety were too much; they had undermined his health. But what could she do? Her brother, she knew, would sooner die than give up his work. She was miserable beyond expression. There was no one to help her; she was alone in the world, without a friend or relative. But no; she was not without a friend. There was her friend Dalton, of whom she had so often thought with love and longing; she would call him. Alvira was about to return to the house when the noise of falling furniture and a wild cry from her brother attracted her to the spot. Suddenly she saw Mort come from the "Clinic," a long knife in his hand, and, walking backwards, followed by Dr. Clinton, whom he sought to keep at a distance. Alvira being concealed behind the door, held on to it to support herself. The sight had made her faint.

"Keep away from me, Dr. Clinton, or I'll run this knife into you. Not one step, I say. Don't commit any foolishness.

You could not kill me quick enough to prevent me from giving you away. I tell you, have a care!"

Alvira could stand it no longer. Satisfied that her brother did not follow his servant, she slipped behind a bush and ran into the house. Quickly she wrote a few lines to George Dalton, asking him to come to her house, either that very evening or the following morning. She was so excited and nervous that she frequently paused in writing. The note being written and sealed, she hastened into the street, and luckily finding a boy, gave him half a dollar to carry the note to George Dalton's office.

But all this had completely exhausted her strength. She barely managed to reach the library, when she fell upon the lounge, shaken by cold and fever. She had not been in there more than half an hour when the door was opened and Dr. Clinton came in. It was already dark, and he did not see his sister. He ran up and down, gesticulating and fighting imaginary foes. He was striking at one of those phantoms, when he was startled by a sigh. He was so scared that he stood as if rooted to the spot.

"Is it you, Alvira?" he asked, quite unnerved. But being answered by another sigh, he lighted a candle and stepped up to the lounge.

"For God's sake! you have the fever," he cried, in terrible excitement. But he soon mastered himself. Covering her with a heavy blanket, he hastened into the kitchen and made her a hot drink. When Alvira's fever had quieted down, he sat by her side, her hand in his. Once in a while his eyes became restless, and his hand moved toward the vest pocket where his "injector" was. Alvira, who felt much better, smiled at her brother gratefully.

"You have the fever," said her brother.

"Whose fever,—yours?" Alvira asked, frightened.

Dr. Clinton made no answer, but he gazed at her absently.

"This would be a fine affair for you and science if you were to find the very case you were after in your own house. You could be proud of your sister, Alfred."

Clinton stared at her with eyes wide open. "Is it possible, Alvira, that your thoughts could take such sublime flights? You, of all people, could comprehend me and my work? Alvira, I am your brother! Do you suppose I would sacrifice my own sister?"

"Keep quiet, dear," said Alvira, "I shall be all right to-morrow morning. Keep quiet, that you don't get sick yourself. I have not your fever, have I?"

Dr. Clinton had the thumb and index of his right hand in his vest pocket, where he toyed with his instrument, as was his habit.

"This would have been one of those tragic conflicts," said Dr. Clinton, still toying with his hypodermic needle, "if a loving brother could reach the highest aim of his life by the death of his own sister. Don't be frightened, Alvira; it is but one of those crazy questions which doctors are apt to ask. But why should it not be reality? Why should a girl not be permitted to sacrifice her life in the same manner as we? We sacrifice our life to science, and with our lives our pleasures, our youth, and all our desires. Every drop of blood, every fiber of our brain, labors for science, and thus our whole life is one chain of denials, abnegations, and sacrifices. Why should not a girl take that one brave step for the sake of science, which alone would place her on a level with the greatest of men?"

"You look quite tired, dear," said Alvira. "Follow my advice, and take a dose of morphine and go to bed. I feel sick. I would like to sleep a little, if possible."

"You are right," said Clinton, gathering his energy. "A morphine injection will do me good, and, come to think of it, you, too, would sleep better if you had one. You would, in fact, not be able to sleep at all without it," and drawing himself up to his full height, he continued, resolutely, "I will fetch the necessary articles from my room."

He left the room with a heavy tread.

V.

"Did you hear the latest?" said a physician to George Dalton as the two were walking towards the latter's office.

"No," said Dalton; "what is it?"

The physician handed Dalton a medical journal, which contained a full description of the peculiar disease discovered by Dr. Clinton. The writer stated that he had succeeded in discovering the germ as entirely independent of the person ill with the fever. He had brought this independent fever germ to its highest strength in virulence, and then weakened it so that it became absolutely harmless. All this he had tested by experiment on animals, and demonstrated publicly, and while Dr. Clinton had certainly given an impetus to investigation, he had achieved nothing new.

"This will bring Dr. Clinton down a peg or two," said the disciple of Esculapius, not without malice.

Dalton's heart was heavy as he stepped into his private office, and he experienced something of a shock when his office-boy handed him Alvira's note. He lost no time, but hastened to the call of the woman he had loved these many years.

"I am so glad you have come," said Alvira, after telling him of all that had transpired within the last few hours.

"And where is your brother now?" Dalton inquired.

"He has just gone down to get me a morphine injection. I think he is right. I shall not be able to sleep without it."

"And did he give you nothing else against the fever? Did he give you any medicine?" asked Dalton.

"No; he don't believe much in medicines," said Alvira. "I will be all right soon. Are you going to leave me now?" she asked, seeing Dalton rise.

"I am going to see your brother," the latter replied, resolutely.

"That is right," said Alvira. "But be

patient with him, for my sake, and, above all things, try and excuse your presence in the house."

Dalton left the room. He stepped down hastily, and as he turned to the Doctor's room he noticed the light coming through the open door. Dalton halted and looked into the room. At the table sat Dr. Clinton, staring into the light. Before him lay an open book in which he had evidently been writing; his right hand held a pen, and his left toyed with the golden injector. Dalton entered, and as Dr. Clinton recognized his visitor, he jumped from his chair and said: "My sister has a slight attack of fever. I was afraid she might grow worse, and concluded to give her an injection of morphine, which I had just now chemically tested. Remedies like those require the greatest care."

He had evidently forgotten how he had

dismissed his sister's suitor. Clinton's words, at first full of embarrassment, grew rather mocking in tone at the end. Dalton lost all control of himself. His eyes involuntarily fell upon the book, and there, in the Doctor's large, bold handwriting, stood the date of the day, the month, and the year, and beneath it, in red ink, the words *8:30 P. M., last trial.* Clinton turned toward the door, and was about to leave, but Dalton barred his way.

"Can you give me your word of honor, Dr. Clinton, that this injection will do your sister no harm?"

Dalton said this in a hoarse voice. Clinton was stunned at Dalton's words, but he soon regained his composure and his mocking tone: "This remedy is reliable, I assure you."

But, suddenly changing his tone, he said: "May I ask the reason of your visit at such a late hour, Mr. Dalton? I had an idea that we had done with each other for life."

Dalton kept an eye on Clinton. Taking the medical journal containing the article against the "Fever" from his pocket, Dalton spoke in measured tones: "In this journal, Dr. Clinton, you will find an article which is of the greatest importance to you, as it affects your lifelong labors. Read it."

Under the pressure of Dalton's gaze, Clinton looked at the journal. He had hardly read the heading of the article when he turned deathly pale. The hand that held the hypodermic syringe trembled, and, totally unnerved, he sank into a chair. Clinton read the article, and after he had finished, he heaved a deep sigh, like one who has received a death-blow. He looked at Dalton as if he desired to read the latter's thoughts. Dalton could barely stand this look, for he felt as if he had spoken Dr.

Clinton's death-sentence. Suddenly Clinton rose from his seat, stepped to the other side of the big table, so that the table was between him and Dalton. His eyes shone with radiance that beautified his face.

"You have asked me a while ago whether I would pledge my honor upon the reliability of this remedy. I will pledge my life." Dr. Clinton had taken hold of the loose skin on his neck, and before Dalton could move, injected the contents of the syringe. At first Dalton was paralyzed, but he soon ran up to Dr. Clinton and tore the injector from the latter's hand. It was too late. Clinton tried to make light of the matter, saying that he only meant to scare Dalton; but when he saw the latter's despair, his bravado gave way to a like feeling. With a cry of horror he threw himself on Dalton's breast and said: "For God's sake, George, save Alvira. I am lost, but you will spare me for her sake."

"I will," said Dalton; "and now lie down and rest. I think you will need to. I will look after Alvira."

Slowly Dalton went upstairs again, so as to collect himself, and not to frighten Alvira by his looks. He told the girl not to despair about her brother; that he was all right, and except the interruption caused by some physical disarrangement, will continue his work. However, he thought it advisable that Alvira should look after her brother once in a while, and for that purpose she must try to get well soon. He also said that he had made up with her brother, and that he would now call more frequently, after which he left her in a blissful deception, but himself heartsore and troubled.

Two days passed. Dalton came twice a day, and Alvira's reports were quite encouraging. "Her brother felt tired," she said. "He writes everything in his book of scientific notes,—his pulse, his temperature. To me he is quite tender, and he is full of praise about your manliness and worth"; and the girl smiled as a woman only can smile when proud of the man she loves.

On the third day a frightful fever attacked Dr. Clinton. His sister watched by his side during the day, and at night Dalton changed with Mort. Upon a little table near the bed was the day-journal in which Clinton wrote notes as often as he was clear-headed. During the day, while his sister was by his side, he seldom uttered a word; his power of will seemed strong enough, even in the heat of fever. He would not shock the poor girl. But it was different before the men. Now he seemed to be among the Mexicans, whom he gave snakes. "They are good; they don't bite;

eat them, eat them!" he cried. Then, again, he seemed to be in the West Indies, where he and Mort were hunting patients. But he could not find them; and if he did not find them within a specified time, he would be hanged. The library seemed full of laughing and grinning doctors, howling dogs, and gnawing rats. He was looking for his great book upon the "Fever Bacillus," which he could not find. Some one of the grinning doctors had stolen it, trying to rob him of his fame.

When Dalton heard these ravings, he shuddered and disliked to stay. But when Mort came into the room, and Dalton saw that moving skeleton grin and leer at the poor Doctor, he was loath to leave him alone with that abominable wretch.

Five days had gone by. Clinton was still raving. Dalton sat by his side, contemplating the sad end of a brilliant career, when Clinton suddenly sat up in his bed. "George, promise me," he said, and his words came hard and slow. "It will be too late to-morrow. Send this book to the fellow who wrote that article. Let him use it."

"If this book is so valuable, why not publish it for Alvira's benefit?" asked Dalton.

"No, no!" cried Clinton. "I have worked for science only. Everything for science; for humanity, nothing. If you don't send it, destroy it. Another thing, George: in Mort's 'Clinic' over there, — in the glass tubes, — all the diseases in the world are in those tubes. There are the 'Fever Bacilli.' I want rest in the grave. They will come from those tubes and destroy mankind to the last. Swear, Dalton, that you will destroy them —"

"How are the poisons to be destroyed?" Dalton faltered.

"By fire, by fire, by fire!" screamed Clinton. "Otherwise that fellow Mort is sure to come and carry the diseases and death among the people. He was always so hard against my dog Bruno, — I have no time now. I am looking for fresh subjects. I want to make my last injection. Ha, ha, ha! I am the creator of the fever! The fools did not know it, — one more"; and Clinton became again delirious.

About two o'clock in the morning Mort entered and desired to take Dalton's place, but the latter remained until daybreak. When he left he heard Clinton cry, "Burn them, Dalton, and Mort, too."

Dalton was gone about two hours, and was about to lie down to rest for a little while when the fire alarm was sounded. Looking out of the window, he saw the flames rising from the direction of Dr. Clinton's house. He dressed hastily and went thither. Dalton found Alvira wringing her hands in front of Mort's "Clinic," which was being consumed in spite of all efforts of the firemen. The house, being quite a distance from the "Clinic," was not in danger.

"Where is your brother?" cried Dalton.

"I don't know," answered the weeping girl. "I went to his room some time ago and found him and Mort gone."

In the afternoon the firemen found the charred remains of two bodies lying upon the stone floor of the "Clinic."

Dalton examined them and identified his poor friend Dr. Clinton, as well as his evil genius, Mort. In the breast of the latter was found a long Persian dagger.

THE FOREIGN ELEMENT.

I.

AWAY out in that part of the Mission, in San Francisco, known as the "Warm Belt" lives a little Irishman who goes by the name of the "Patriarch," although his right name is Patrick O'Hara. There is certainly nothing patriarchal, pious, or heaven-striving about the man's features or appearance, unless it be the point of his nose, which has a decided upward tilt; otherwise one is not reminded of O'Hara's devotional proclivities. He swears sometimes, but as his imprecations are usually directed against the "*Oppressor*," one does not take it to heart.

O'Hara is rich. He owns considerable

property in the Mission, and he does not work. But this is not the reason why they style him the "Patriarch."

"You see that little man there," said the clerk at the corner grocery; "that's him."

"Who?" I queried.

"The fellow we was talking about,—the Patriarch," he replied.

"But why is he called the Patriarch?" I asked.

"Because he has twelve sons and four daughters," replied the clerk.

"Twelve sons and four daughters!" I cried. The clerk must have thought me crazy, as I ran out of the grocery and raced after Pat O'Hara. I wanted to shake hands with the man who could boast the progeny of twelve solid Democratic citizens, adding four votes when Lizzie, Maggie, Mary Ann, and Katie should have found their masculine equals among the aristocratic families of the "Warm Belt."

Having caught up with Mr. O'Hara, I asked the privilege of shaking him by the hand.

"Faith, if that'll do yez any good, ye are welcome," he said, with a grin.

I assured him that it would make me quite happy.

"Then do it agin," said he, and he held forth his big, horny hand.

"Phfat may be yer business?" he queried.

"I am a reporter," I replied.

"I hope ye dun't wroite for any of thim Ripublican papers," he said, and gazed at his hand, evidently regretting that he had shaken hands too hastily.

I assured him that I was a stanch Democrat, and would not bemean myself by writing for a Republican journal.

"Then shake," said Pat, quite happy. "Ye are the man I loike."

THE FOREIGN ELEMENT. 219

As he spoke, I had a chance to take a mental photograph of the man who lived up to his principles, even to the shaking of hands.

His eyes — blue in color and small in circumference — had the merriest twinkle imaginable. There seemed an eternal grin about his mouth, but I was inclined to think — after close inspection — that the grin was due to the natural cut of his mouth, the sides of which terminated in the back. He had teeth, too, but the lips seemed ashamed of them, for they made ineffectual efforts to cover them. Between the teeth a clay pipe had taken permanent lodgings, never leaving, rain or shine. As for Mr. O'Hara's hair and chin whiskers, they were, as usual, of the flaming color.

"So you are the father of sixteen children, Mr. O'Hara," I said.

"Yes, sure, I have the foinest b'ys in the

country, sur, an' foiner gurls ye can't find in the wurld," he said, with all the pride he could possibly put into his words.

"How old is your oldest child, Mr. O'Hara?"

"Me oldest son will be tirty-tree next Christmas, sur."

"And your youngest?"

"Is here,—right here, sur. An' as foin a gurl as iver ye laid eyes on. Kathy, darlint, come here; come here an' shake hands with the gintleman."

Kathy came and shook hands. Her hands were rather dirty, but her sweet face and rich carnation atoned for the insufficient use of soap and water. Kathy was about six years of age. Maggie, the oldest, was about twenty; then came Lizzie, eighteen, and Mary Ann, sixteen years of age.

Lizzie was certainly the handsomest of

all the girls. She was, in fact, very beautiful.

"It costs something to bring up a family like yours, Mr. O'Hara?" said I.

"Yes, sur; it does cost a little something," he replied, sucking at his clay pipe. "But there's enough for all, an' some to spare. Me childhren can hav' anything they want. All I ask in return is for thim to kape clane the reckord. They must marry none but Irish gurls, an' me gurls shall marry Irish b'ys."

Interesting as the study of this phase of the Irish character would have been, I forebore the pleasure, bade Mr. O'Hara a "good day," and left.

II.

Several weeks later, I again happened to meet Mr. O'Hara. His nose was still in the same position; his eyes were blue, but they had lost the merry twinkle; the upper lip was drawn tightly over his upper teeth, in a vain endeavor to meet the lower lip. The latter hung down listless, and in the corners there was a glimmer of white foam. Patrick O'Hara was evidently a broken-down and unhappy man. Touched by a humane impulse, I walked up to him and, taking him by the hand, said:—

"What seems to be the matter, Mr. O'Hara?"

His lower lip trembled as he recognized me.

"Iverything is the matter," he breathed.

I took a seat by his side.

"It is the 'grippe,' Mr. O'Hara," I said. "You will be all right soon. Brace up. A man who has twelve brave boys and four handsome girls has cause to be happy."

"There is no happy days fur me any

mohre," he said. There was a deep note of sadness and melancholy in his voice. "I hav' no luck, sur. Me ouldest b'y married an English gurl, and me second ran away with a Dutch bar-maid. The foreign iliment, sur, is what kills this grate country, an' it is the foreign iliment that kills the family. I have no luck, sur."

At this juncture little Kathy came racing through the yard, and cried: "Pop, I have a nickel and a box of candy."

She handed the box of candy to her father, who gazed into it sadly, extracted a piece and slipped it into his capacious, mouth, and then offered me the box. I refused, with thanks, but asked Kathy who had given her the candy.

"Mr. Isaak," she said.

"Do you like Mr. Isaak?" I asked.

"Yes, I do," she replied.

"And would you like me if I gave you candy and a nickel?" I queried.

She thought a while; then she said, "No; you ain't Lizzie's beau, and Mr. Isaak is."

If a cannon had been discharged full at the breast of Mr. O'Hara, the effect could not have been more terrific. His eyes shot sparks, the foam in the corners of his mouth spread and filled the aperture with a film thereof.

"Kathy, darlint, come here, acushla," he cried. "What did you say was the name of the chap who is Lizzie's beau?"

"His name is Mr. Isaak. The boys call him 'Sheeny Jake,'" she said, munching her candy, unconscious of the agony she was causing her father. The blow was too hard for him of the O'Hara race. He took his head between his hands, bent it between his knees, and set up a moaning that would have turned Lizzie's callous heart, had she heard it.

As it was, her father uttered groan after groan, such as come from the breast of a true Irishman in despair, while the wayward Lizzie was cooing in the arms of her Hebrew lover, whose father sold notions, and he himself earned the princely salary of forty dollars per month in one of the great bazars of San Francisco.

I tried to console poor O'Hara. "He may be a good young man. The Jews have a reputation of treating their wives much better than Christians. He may make Lizzie quite happy, and it ought to be your pride to see your children happy."

"Och, Mr. Martin, ye are not married. Ye did n't have the trouble av bringing up sixteen childhren. Am I to slave for me childhren's happiness, an' as soon as they grow up, fur thim to make me unhappy? Oi say, no, sur! An' suppos' he meks her a good husband, will that take off the disgrace of the foreign iliment? Oi say agin, no, sur! To have the oppressor's daughther in me family, and a Dutch bar-maid, is bad enough, but a Jew!—I'll niver live to see the day. No, I won't. If me childhren are bent on disgracing me name, let thim do it when I ain't about."

It seems, however, that Patrick O'Hara did not commit suicide that day. Mrs. O'Hara gave Lizzie a good talking, and she promised that she would not disgrace the family. When he heard his daughter's promise, it pleased him mightily.

"Yez are an honest man's honorable daughter. Yer father is a man av substance; ye can have whativer you like, an' why should yez hang yerself on the neck av an old good-for-nothin' Jew,—an idler who would kape ye in want the rist av yer naturral loife."

"Jake—I mean Mr. Isaak—is no idler,

papa," said Lizzie. "He works and makes his own living; although his people are quite wealthy, he never asks anything of them. He stands on his own legs."

"An' how do ye know all this, Liz?" asked O'Hara.

She turned crimson. "I heard it," she said, and was about to leave the room.

"Lizzie!" cried her father.

Lizzie halted.

"What do you want, pa?"

"Come here."

She obeyed.

"Lizzie, I want ye to promise me not to talk to that Jew Isaak. Not that I distrust me own daughther, but that Jew will mislead you; and if ye iver disgrace me, I shall cut you off from the family. Now, you will have to choose between your family and that Jew Isaak."

"Papa, do you doubt me?" cried Lizzie.

"Well, I am bound to. Ye was seen with him; yer little sister called him yer beau. Now, while it ain't any crime to speak to any gintleman on the street, it is certainly a different affair when it comes to marriage. Marry the poorest lad in the neighborhood, and be sure yer father will stand by ye; but for God's sake don't bring me any foreign iliment."

"I won't, pa," said Lizzie.

"Swear by the Holy Virgin, then, gurl," cried O'Hara.

Poor Lizzie trembled, as she placed her hand upon the bisque statue of the Virgin, and hot tears fell from her lids.

"I swear!" she breathed, and fell into her mother's arms, weeping.

Shortly after this dramatic scene, another — one of joyous moment — took place in the O'Hara residence. Maggie married Tim Ryan, the man who kept a saloon, was a sport, and had the full favor of Patrick O'Hara, inasmuch as he, too, hated the "foreign iliment."

The acquisition of a thoroughbred son of Erin caused Patrick O'Hara to forget all his former troubles.

"Mr. Martin, sur, a sight loike that"— pointing to his son-in-law and Maggie — "is enough to drown all trouble, even if there was no champagne. Drink, sur. I invited yez to see me joy, because ye saw also me sorrow. Drink, sur, an' may God blesh ye."

III.

Tim Ryan became a great factor in the O'Hara establishment. Being shrewd, he soon found out the peculiar weakness of his father-in-law, taking good care to keep his standing. Patrick O'Hara embraced Tim, as the latter told him that

"Sheeny Jake" had tried to speak to Lizzie, but that he (Tim) had threatened to thrash the Jew if he ever dared to insult his sister-in-law.

As a matter of course, however, Tim had not spoken to Lizzie's sweetheart, although he had seen the two in close conversation near the Cogswell Institute.

One bright sunny morning as I was sitting on a bench in a shrubbery in the park, I heard a sob, and a masculine voice say: "Don't cry, Lizzie. I have the same difficulty at home. My father lectures me continually about not marrying out of the faith. He hates mixed marriages, and would not hear of it, unless, indeed, darling, — you would consent to embrace the Jewish faith. You know how my dear mother would love you. They would carry you on their hands, and my old dad — well, there isn't a better chap living, but he will have no foreign element."

"Oh, Jack dear, how can you say this to me? Do you want me to break my poor father's heart? A marriage would be hard enough in his eyes, but to become a traitor to the Church, this he would not forgive; and would you want your wife to be burdened by a father's curse and the everburning tears of a mother? O God," cried Lizzie, — for I knew now that it was Lizzie O'Hara and her lover, Jake Isaak, — "my mother has been so kind to me ever since I was a baby. I was such a care to her, more than any of her children. It hurts my heart to think of it"; and the girl sobbed.

"I am in the same fix, darling," said her lover. "But what can we do? Do you want to give me up, Lizzie?" There was a tremor in his voice as he said this.

"O no," cried she.

"Well, then, there is but one course open

to us. Since you will never gain your folks' consent to a marriage with me, and as my people will consent only on condition that you become a Jewess, — but as I love you too much to ask you to do a cruel thing to your parents, — I propose that we marry by law; and if after a year you still love me as you do now, and you have not obtained your people's forgiveness, I propose that you embrace the faith of the people who will receive you with never-failing love. Are you willing, Lizzie darling?"

I could not hear the answer; but it must have been quite satisfactory to both, judging by the osculatory music that floated in rapid tempo through the shrubbery.

I struck a match and lit a cigar. "The knowledge of a secret makes the heart heavy," is an old saying; but though I knew Mr. Jake Isaak and Miss Lizzie

O'Hara were planning an elopement, I felt light and comfortable; and, what was more, I did not propose to interfere, either. Who knows, how soon I might be in the same fix?—I argued,—and made up my mind to forget that Mr. Patrick O'Hara existed.

Two days later I went North, thence to New York and Europe. I was away some eighteen months.

IV.

On my arrival in San Francisco, I met an old friend, a Jewish merchant.

"Martin," said he, "I know you are interested in Jewish affairs and customs; if you will accompany me to the Turk Street synagogue to-morrow, you shall witness a peculiar ceremony.

On my asking of what nature the ceremony would be, he refused to answer.

"Come and see, — at 10 A. M., sharp," was all he said as he jumped off the car

At ten o'clock the following morning I was at the synagogue impatiently waiting for my Jewish friend. At length he came.

"Now watch," he said; "when the Rabbi opens the ark there, where stands the holy scroll, the ceremony will begin."

I could hardly master myself, I was so impatient to see that peculiar ceremony.

Presently the Rabbi rose and drew aside the heavy velvet curtain, embroidered with massive bullion, in the center being two golden lions supporting a crown. As the curtain moved to the left, the congregation rose. The Rabbi opened the doors of the ark, bent low, and kissed the holy scroll; he then turned toward the congregation and said: "My friends, we are about to perform the novel ceremony of initiating into the holy covenant a mother and her child. The mother, a born Christian, has voluntarily embraced Judaism. I have instructed her, and am proud to state that a truer daughter of Israel will not be found, even among those born in the faith. Leah, rise and proclaim thy faith in the one God of Israel."

At this a young woman, clad in purest white, rose, and with bent head, in her arms an infant, ascended the stairs leading to the ark. The words she spoke—in bell-like notes, sweet and distinct—impressed themselves on my mind: "*Shemang Yisroel adonoi elohenu-adonio echod.*" My friend translated them for me. They are: "Hear, oh Israel, the Lord our God, the Lord is one."

I had recognized Lizzie O'Hara at once. She must have experienced naught but love and affection to act as she did. After her profession of faith the Rabbi took the child from her arms, and lifting it before the ark, said:

"May thy name be called in Israel, Sarah, and may thy parents live to see thee happily married and prosperous. Amen!"

I waited till the service was over, and then offered my congratulations to the beautiful mother convert. She remembered me quite well.

"You kept your promise, made in the Golden Gate Park," I said.

She blushed and smiled. "So it was you, then. I thought I heard some one strike a match," she said.

"Yes; it was I. And where is your father?" I queried.

"My father sold his property and went back to Ireland. He has disinherited me; but I am satisfied; my husband is doing well, and we are happy.

"I am glad for your sake," said I, and left.

V.

Two years had passed, and one day while walking on Kearny Street, I felt a hand on my arm; turning I gazed into the broad, grinning face of Patrick O'Hara.

"When did you come back?" I asked.

"Some toime since," he replied.

"And have you seen your daughter Lizzie?"

"Av course," he said. "We av kissed and med up. I could not live widout me daughther Lizzie."

"And how about that foreign element, Mr. O'Hara?" I asked, with a smile.

"One religion is as good as the other," he said. "An if Oi had known that 'Sheeny Jake'—as they used to call me son-in-law —would make sich a good husband, I would let all me gurls marry 'Sheenies'; so I would, be jabers!"

"That's a pretty baby of your daughter Lizzie," I said.

"Oh, that baby of theirs," said he, in ecstasy, —"it's a perfect darlint, Mr. Martin, — a perfect darlint. You must come and see it. It's so smart. You know, Mr. Martin," he said, standing on tiptoe and whispering into my ear, "I belave it's the mixed breed — the foreign iliment — that makes the kid so smart!"

THE FATAL LETTER.

I.

"OH, madame, madame! I cannot write ze English lettair. I 'av' try; ze is too hard," said Babette, Mrs. Mogens's French maid, holding a pen in her trembling right hand while wiping her brow with the back of her left. She looked the very picture of despair, and the ever-laughing Mrs. Mogens, who had been on the point of ringing one of her merry peals at Babette's exclamation, suppressed her natural inclination, and asked who was the object of her attempted correspondence.

"Zat is Monsieur Morries, my sweetheart, zat I write," explained Babette.

"Where does he live, Babette?" inquired Mrs. Mogens, interested.

"In ze ceety," replied the maid.

"And what would you like to write him?"

"O, he is very nice young man, and I write him zat I look favorable upon his suit,—zat I,"— here Babette blushed to the roots of her hair, —"zat I lofe him."

Now, Mrs. Mogens was just the kind of woman to encourage people in love affairs, no matter what the consequences might be. She would have gone miles to pacify a pouting maiden or bring back a recreant lover. She considered it her special mission in this vale of unhappiness to counteract the set purpose of nature in squeezing the lachrymal glands of human beings. *Happiness* was her watchword; she wanted all people to be happy. Hence her readiness to assist Babette.

"Does Mr. Morris reciprocate your feeling?" inquired Mrs. Mogens.

"*Mon Dieu!* he tell me, yes," said Babette.

"Very well, then, Babette, I will write your letter, and you may copy it and send him the happy message; but, remember, don't send my handwriting; you must copy it.

"*Mille merci*, madame," cried Babette, and, kissing Mrs. Mogens's hand, ran from the room.

Mrs. Mogens went to her elegant writing-desk, took a sheet of finely scented paper, and was about to compose the love-letter, but, not knowing the christian name of Babette's lover, she rang the bell which summoned the maid.

"What is Mr. Morris's christian name?" asked Mrs. Mogens.

"He tell me his name is Petair Morries. I call him Petit,—*Mon Petit;* zat is nice," she said, with a rippling smile.

Mrs. Mogens thought it nice, indeed, and wrote one of those charming notes which are half a confession and half an insinuation, and which would have filled the heart of the most phlegmatic lover with joy and daring. The letter being finished, Mrs. Mogens quite unconsciously signed it, and left it on the table for Babette to copy. She then proceeded to her apartment, made her toilet, and went out.

II.

Mr. Mogens, the husband of Mrs. Mogens, was a peculiar character. He had married late in life. He never told the reason why he had waited so long; but intimate acquaintances said that he was too shy in his youth, and in his manhood too busy to think of matrimony. But every one has his Kismet. Mr. Mogens met Miss Ophelia Love, and this settled his fate. She was tall, beautiful, and bright; she loved pleasure and wealth; and Mr. Mogens thought life and railroad stock far above par, but of little value without Miss Ophelia Love. He proposed; and as his manly manner and good looks were enhanced by half a dozen millions and a mansion on "Nob Hill," Miss Love — being encouraged by her handsome mother — accepted all in one hand. It is necessary to reiterate that Mr. Mogens was good-looking, although his driver called him Mr. Muggins, and Pety Baglow called him Mug, for short.

Mr. Mogens seemed happy and contented; and were it not for a periodical dejection which he strove hard to master, he would have passed for that anomaly in this world of care, — a happy rich man. This periodical dejection was not caused by fluctuations in the stock market, nor by the rumored unstability of banks; neither by annoying neighbors nor by political opponents, for Mr. Mogens's fortune, as was already pointed out, was secure, and his mansion, with gardens, occupied a whole block. Nor would Mr. Mogens have accepted a United States senatorship if the people had thrown it at his feet; he was patriotic in a Mogenesque fashion, but he loathed politics. His sole anxiety — it might as well be told now — was his wife, the vivacious Mrs. Mogens. Yes, Ophelia Mogens — Ophelia Love, her intimates called her — was, ever since she came to her husband's stately mansion, a source of pleasure and palpitation to the otherwise serene heart that beat in the manly Mogens bosom.

The trouble with her — or rather with him — was his wife's superlative beauty.

THE FATAL LETTER. 245

Mr. Mogens thought of the many snares and pitfalls a mashing Kearny Street world presented to a beautiful woman walking unattended amidst the multitude. Ah, if Mrs. Mogens possessed that shielding quality — some call it virtue — of shyness, the bejeweled and ogling masher might founder on such a rock! But Mrs. Mogens held her head high when she essayed on one of her "down-town walks." She even looked the masher straight in the face; but her pure gaze and invulnerable virtue caused brazen sin to beat an ignominious retreat to the accommodating cigar-store. The masher's head invariably drooped before her imperious look; and when his red nose touched the flashing diamond on his shirt-front, Mrs. Mogens smiled, — a smile such as angels would over the triumph of a saint.

But Mr. Mogens understood her not.

He saw only her smile, and this smile, he thought, was enough to encourage the angel Gabriel to sell his famous trumpet for old brass, and to enter into a partnership with his Nickish Majesty of the Pit. When Mr. Mogens accompanied his wife down town, therefore, he suffered the most exquisite torture, and his eyes — from a forced endeavor to reconnoiter both sides of the sidewalk — had actually acquired that peculiar expression which is said to belong to those whose right eye looks for Christmas when the left is looking for Easter Sunday. And when Mrs. Mogens — at such queer moments — looked at her husband's queer eyes, her silver smile broke into a golden laugh. Mr. Mogens, like all well-bred slaves, gave his eyes a convulsive jerk, sighed, and said — nothing. But in his heart — for Mr. Mogens had a heart, a pious, loving, throbbing heart — in his heart he was sad and dejected.

After all, what could he do? He could not lock her up in the house. He had thought of such an expedient once, but the thought did not fecundate, because Mrs. Mogens had once remarked that if she had had the misfortune to marry a man who would restrict her, and not such a darling as Mr. Mogens, she would have committed suicide the first opportunity she should have had. At these words, which seemed to have answered his incipient resolution to lock her up, Mr. Mogens shivered and kissed his wife's hand. What a beautiful hand hers was! so finely shaped, so small and full; and the skin was as soft as that of an infant. As he gazed upon that alabaster-like hand, and thought that this very hand might be discolored and shriveled by a self-inflicted death, he felt a cold, creepy sensation down his spine and a chill in his bones. No; he would do nothing that might possibly deprive him of this hand, and his eyes from feasting upon the glorious beauty of her face and form.

And so he sighed, and concluded to bear his burden manfully. She was his wife, after all, — his, and his only. Besides, he had the satisfaction of not being bored by too many visitors and a chance lover. The few elderly ladies and gentlemen who were entertained once or twice a week could hardly be called dangerous. There was nothing to be apprehended on this score; and in his house, at least, Mr. Mogens had no cause for anxiety.

But his heart was doomed to a long martyrdom. For, one bright November day, as Mr. and Mrs. Mogens were walking on Market Street they were met by two tall gentlemen, and one of them said, "Hello, Mug, old man, how are you?" and, taking off his hat, he continued, addressing Mrs. Mogens, " This is my friend, Mr. Bearspaw." Mrs. Mogens was exceedingly glad to meet Mr. Bearspaw; she had read his writings, and admired him very much. Mr. Bearspaw's usual severity vanished in the presence of Mrs. Mogens; and, though he was not given to answering any questions that any one, male or female, might ask, he very soon found himself answering some propounded by the charming Mrs. Mogens; which demonstrates that there never yet lived a philosopher who was impervious to a woman's charms, especially when the woman had spirit, and plenty of that woman's sense known as " tact."

Mr. Bearspaw was, as already indicated, tall and finely proportioned. He had a military carriage, and the face of a thinker. His features were strong and marked; not that there was that cadaverous hollowness

in his face that sometimes gives intellectual
people a satanic look, but the strength was
rather marked in the general make-up of
that remarkable face. His forehead had
long, deep lines, and his brows were of an
extraordinary length. But, while they
partly shadowed, they did not prevent the
observer from seeing a most penetrating
eye, blue in color, but by its great sharp-
ness robbed of that insipidness which gen-
erally marks eyes of "heavenly hue." A
straight nose added to the character of the
face, and an elegantly shaped mustache
completed it. He spoke in a low tone of
voice, and in this, probably, was the only
fault of the man's make-up. There was no
strength in it; he seemed afraid to speak;
but he only seemed so, for, in reality, there
was nothing in how loud he said a thing,
but *what* he said, and that carried weight
every time. As he walked by the side

of Mrs. Mogens, they appeared a very handsome pair, the whole strength of his manhood matched against her glorious womanhood.

Mr. Mogens's heart gave a thump as he saw his wife look up to Mr. Bearspaw's face with an intensity that was as new as it was startling. And Bearspaw looked down into her face and smiled. Bearspaw looked dreadful when he frowned, but when he smiled,— well, that was quite a different affair.

"The devil take —" that was the beginning of Mr. Mogens's sentence, but he only thought those three words; aloud, however, he said, "Your friend there —"

"Yes, isn't he a charming fellow?" interrupted Mr. Pety Baglow. "He is a most delightful fellow. Say, Mug, old boy, I'll bring him up to your house some evening,— say next Sunday evening; will that suit you? I am sure your wife will be de-

lighted to see him. You have still that
good whisky of yours, have n't you?"

And Mr. Mogens said Yes. Thus the
matter was settled, and Pety Baglow raced
on on another theme, so that poor Mr. Mogens's head was in a whirl. He forgot to
look cross-eyed on the sidewalk; all he
knew was that Baglow rattled on, saying
sweet nothings about theater parties and
dinners, and wines and girls, and that in
front of him, like lovers in sweet forgetful-
ness, walked Bearspaw and his Ophelia.
He could have strangled Pety Baglow and
turned a dagger in the entrails of Bearspaw.
Oh, how he regretted not having realized
that first thought of shutting her up in the
house! But he recalled her threatened
suicide in a given case, and he mastered his
rage,— sighed, and bore his burden with
Christian meekness. But fate is sometimes
better than man imagines. Did Pety see

the poor man's sufferings, and desire to pour oil into the wound? or was it merely a natural inclination to tell a pleasant lie? Enough; he told Mr. Mogens that Mr. Bearspaw hated women, and that the impression the sweetest woman would leave in his heart would be a desire to never meet her again.

These words had a startling effect upon Mr. Mogens; he became positively lively, and linked his arm with that of Baglow. The recording angel sneezed, so that a drop of heavenly saliva fell on the book, and Pety had a notch to his credit. Of course, Pety told Mr. Mogens that he (Pety) was not as unsusceptible as Bearspaw, but Mogens laughed at the thought of Pety's rivalry. He knew him too well; good old Pety, — he would have trusted him with everything, excepting, perhaps, his Ophelia, — but this was quite a different matter.

As a matter of course, however, Mr. Mogens underrated Pety Baglow's quality in "stooping to conquer." Because Pety Baglow was a student of the gentler sex, and though all fish was not meat to him, yet when a man is hunting up authorities on the "Art of Persuasion," he must, of necessity, give the material on hand a fair trial, and Baglow's trials were nearly always of the fair kind. Might he not be induced — simply from love of study — to change the subject? — physicians certainly do so quite often, and Pety was a student of anatomy from no motive of gain, but for the love of the thing. His endeavors had been crowned with exceptional success in nearly every instance; and though he was a student and a writer of repute, he was not at all pedantic. To be sure, his nature was in total opposition to that of Bearspaw; but all people cannot be alike. Pety was as light as air, but he was beautiful. One would not have called him handsome, because this term applies to persons of a grosser nature. Pety's nature was fine; he was born of a woman, brought up among women, and he needed woman's sympathy and woman's love to spice his life. In this intercourse he had acquired all the *finesse* of a woman; his touch was tender and delicate; his manner gentle. Had he been beardless, his oval face and soft, pointed chin, his long hair and dreamy eyes, would have given him the character of a beautiful woman. His rich red and swelling lips might have stamped him a voluptuous woman. But as he was a man, — with a certain man's courage, and the qualifying masculine hairiness, — it made him what women were pleased to call a beautiful man. His mustache covered his upper lip, according to regulation, and a short, pointed beard toned up his feminine chin. He was a favorite with men, and more so with women. His gentle manner, his pretty speech, his readiness to do them favors, — small favors, to be sure, such as not even jealous husbands would object to, — captivated them. Mr. Baglow was a fortunate man, indeed.

III.

"Good by, Mr. Baglow, and call again," said Mrs. Mogens, opening the door.

"Thanks, awfully," replied Mr. Baglow, and bowed himself out. But he bowed himself into the avoirdupois of Mr. Mogens, who was nearly knocked down from the steps leading to his own house.

"Hello, Pety, look out!" cried Mr. Mogens, grabbing the former's coat, by which he managed to gain his equilibrium.

"Beg pardon, old man. How are you?

Charming flowers you have in your garden. By by!" and, skipping down the stairs, he was gone.

At the collision between Mr. Baglow's back and Mr. Mogens's front, Mrs. Mogens uttered a ringing laugh. Mr. Mogens would have frowned if he had dared; as it was, he smiled a sickly sort of a smile, and, entering, kissed his wife on the forehead.

Mr. Baglow had called as promised, but he had come without Mr. Bearspaw. Mrs. Mogens had shown her displeasure almost as much as Mr. Mogens his delight. He hated that Mr. Bearspaw, into whose face his Ophelia had looked with so much evident pleasure. Mr. Mogens was so happy at the absence of the supposed rival that Pety Baglow's attentions to his wife evoked but little feeling. But Mr. Baglow had continued his visits at short intervals. He brought flowers, books, and often box-checks for first nights at the Baldwin Theatre. Mr. Mogens was annoyed at first, then suspicious, until the torture became so poignant that he felt sick at heart. He was sure his wife liked Pety Baglow; he had seen her smile upon him — oh, so happily! She had never smiled on him — her own husband, her benefactor — so sweetly. Each smile cut his heart; but what could he do? Of course, he might have ordered Pety Baglow from the house; but what good would that have done him? Might they not carry on their illicit love somewhere else? It is an old saying, that those bent on mischief laugh at watchfulness. He could do nothing.

Several days later, as Mr. Mogens ascended the steps leading to his mansion, and thought of the late collision with his hated friend Pety, he kept close to the railing. But he was spared the agony;

the catastrophe did not come to pass. On inquiry, Babette told him that "ze Madame Mogens hav' gon' out." That did not make him any happier. Where had she gone to? Whom had she gone to meet? These were torturing questions. Mr. Mogens lighted a cigar and seated himself at the window. Was he going to spy on his wife? Probably. But who would not excuse him? He worshiped her; there on the wall hung her picture, — what a grand woman she was! Suddenly he felt a desire to go into her boudoir, to see her trinkets, to kiss everything his wife had looked at or touched. Oh, was there ever such a love as burned in his tortured heart?

He opened the door of his wife's room and looked in. It was the bower of a princess. He entered, and seated himself in a soft chair, — probably the one she had sat in before she had gone out. Suddenly his eye fell upon a sheet of paper on the table, — there was writing on it; he recognized his wife's hand at a glance. To whom had she been writing? Who? Who? An unconquerable desire to read that note seized him. Twice he tried to master his unmanly desire, but at last he succumbed. With a bound he was at the table, — he held the note in his hand, but the hand trembled so he could not see. He heaved a sigh and steadied himself. He needed all the fortitude to remain on his feet; for what he read crushed him to death. A cry of agony escaped his lips; he sank into a chair, but he did not lose consciousness: fate was too cruel for that. There, black on white, was his wife's guilt. "My darling Peter," the letter began, and ended with an effusion of love that drove him mad. Nor had she made any attempt to conceal the fact; she had written that incriminating letter, and had signed it with her — no, his name. He was disgraced, annihilated.

"My darling Peter," she calls him, he murmured at length. "She hopes soon to be his wife; all it needs is to put me out of the way. Very well, Pety, you have wrecked my life, I'll give you a show to wreck hers, also. You shall have her. Life is not worth living if you have to fight for each inch of ground. I am going, I am going"; saying which he left his wife's room and the house.

IV.

Monsieur Morris, the intended husband of Babette, was a charming young man, just such as would capture the heart of a French maid; he was employed in an office that closed its doors daily at two, P. M., and Mr. Morris had all the pleasant afternoon hours to himself. He spent them mostly at the Golden Gate Park. It was there that he met and learned to love his sweet Babette. But if his passion for pretty French maids was bound to end in that derogation of freedom called matrimony, his greater passion for picking choice flowers at the city's park was bound to land him in jail. But Morris indulged in both those passions with a *nonchalance* that was lordly, to say the least. Another peculiarity of Mr. Morris was the wearing of a green coat and a green felt hat, and with his black mustache and beard *a la* Napoleon the Third, he looked not unlike his club-footed Majesty at a ball. "Every crime has its time," is a saying, and Mr. Morris's predilection for stealing flowers brought him into unpleasant relations with the park police.

It was on the day that Babette sent him the happy message of her love that Mr.

Morris, dressed in a bright green coat and hat, walked jauntily into the Park, whistling a few bars from that charming opera, "Cavalleria Rusticana." A beautiful oleander-blossom took his fancy, and, without much care for spying policemen, he broke it off and put it into his buttonhole. But the Argus-eye of an officer was upon him; to be sure, the policeman was a quarter of a mile away, but as he made straight for Mr. Morris, the latter thought speed the better part of valor. He cut and ran into the depth of a bush, and had the satisfaction of seeing the policeman race by at the top of his speed. He knew that the police would beat the bush and find him erelong; he also knew that he would go to jail, and this was not quite agreeable, when one anticipates matrimony in a few days. He thought of means to get out of the Park unobserved; but he looked at his green coat, — the police would recognize that a mile off, — and he despaired. Suddenly he heard a voice, and as he looked to his right, he saw a man.

"I am tired of this everlasting torture," said the man. "I'll make an end of it."

Mr. Morris was about to say "Don't," being afraid that the man might expedite his soul by means of lead and powder, which would attract those "hounds of justice," as he styled the reputable persons who follow the shrill call of the police-whistle. But, to his great relief, he saw the man take a bottle from his pocket, which he could see was labeled "*laudanum*," and deliberately drink it contents. A happy thought struck Morris, and he smiled with satisfaction. Bending over the twigs, he stepped into the place where the suicide lay.

"See here, friend," said Morris, "I saw you drink that stuff; in twenty minutes you will be as dead as a door-nail. The police are after me for stealing flowers in this park. I cannot leave the place with this green coat and hat; give me yours while there is time, and you put on mine. You will save me from trouble and my Babette from anxiety, for, let me tell you, sir, I shall be married in a week, and I don't like to go to jail just now."

When the suicide heard that Morris was about to get married, he smiled, and said, "I have half a mind to let those fellows arrest you; the confinement in the county jail would probably cure your attempted matrimonial folly. But, as you seem to be bent upon mischief, have your own way"; saying which, he took off his coat and hat and donned those of Morris. The exchange was hardly made when the police were upon them.

"There he is, the fellow in the green

coat," cried the policeman who had chased Morris.

"That man has committed suicide, gentlemen," said Morris, gravely. "You had better ring up a patrol wagon"; and in the excitement that followed his statement, he stole away.

V.

Mrs. Mogens felt very uneasy when the dinner-bell rang and her husband had not come home. He was always punctual; what could possibly have kept him out so late? From Babette she had heard that the master had been in, and had gone away again. And it was the first time in her married life that she sat down to dinner alone. Her husband must have found something or somebody very interesting to neglect her thus; she was piqued, for, as a matter of fact, she loved her husband dearly; he was manly and devoted; he always read her wishes from her eyes, and fulfilled them before they were uttered. She mentally compared him with all the men she knew; there was not one she would have put in his place. And then, too, there was the fifth anniversary of their wedding, which was also his birthday. How she had schemed to surprise him, — and now he was neglecting her; that was a sad beginning for the coming joy.

The dinner remained untouched, and when, at midnight, her husband had not returned, Mrs. Mogens, for the first time in her married life, wept and cried herself to sleep. The next morning she was much sadder. Mr. Mogens was not in his apartments, — had not been there at all. The poor woman was nearly frantic; she cried, and Babette cried with her. What were they to do? Mrs. Mogens sent Babette down town to the office; he was not there. At length the bell rang, and the servant announced Mr. Pety Baglow. He appeared to the poor woman like an angel from heaven. If any one, he could find out what had become of Mr. Mogens. When Baglow heard the terrible story, he thought a while; then he thought that Mr. Mogens might have gone the way of all flesh, in one of the many pleasant resorts of San Francisco, where champagne fizzes and semi-dressed women wear sparkling diamonds and play the piano. So Mr. Baglow consoled Mrs. Mogens, and told her that he would go and find her husband (more dead than alive, he added, mentally), and that he would return soon.

Now, Mr. Baglow was an adept in locating all sorts of people, from a lad who ran away from the Boys' and Girls' Aid Society to the bold, bad men who rob trains and kill people because they are too forward in pressing their acquaintance. And so Mr. Baglow scoured the resorts, high and low, but no trace could he find of the missing Mr. Mogens; and as Pety could not bring it over his heart to face a woman when he had to make a discouraging report, he went to a friend whose whisky was better than his reputation, and drowned his failure in copious draughts.

VI.

"Prisoner at the bar, stand up," said Police Judge Hishornblower. The prisoner at the bar looked pale and distinguished. He wore a green coat, which made his face ghastly looking, and on the bench by his side was a green hat.

"You are guilty of a misdemeanor; you are accused of having stolen flowers in the park. Do you plead guilty?"

The prisoner at the bar said he was not guilty.

"Call the witness," cried his Honor.

The witness was called, sworn, and said that his name was Michael McGinnis, a park policeman.

"Is that the man you saw picking flowers?" asked the judge.

"Av yer 'Onor plase, it is th' mon. He had on a grane coht, an' Oi knows grane whin Oi sae it."

The judge was about to sentence the culprit, when an auditor rose and asked permission to address the court. Permission being given, the auditor declared that he was in the park at the time; that he saw the thief, and that he was positive it was a much smaller man who took the flowers. He also maintained that if he put on that green coat and hat, the policeman would accuse him. In fact, he was positive, he stated, that the policeman was under the influence of liquor. The policeman turned purple in the face, and said that if the auditor would put on that coat and hat he would take an oath that he was not the thief.

The judge actually asked the auditor to put on the green coat and hat, and to stand at a distance from the witness. When that was done, the policeman trembled in every limb.

"Av yer 'Onor plase, this mon is the divil, fer, be the saints, it's him Oi saw stealin' thim flowers," cried the policeman, and sat down, stunned.

There was first a titter, then a roar of laughter among the spectators, for the man in the green coat and hat, with his black mustache and pointed beard, looked very much like Mephistopheles in "Faust." Even the judge made but little endeavor to hide his mirth, when suddenly a woman's voice was heard, who said, "*Oh, mon cher Petair!*" It was Babette, who at this moment entered the court-room and espied her lover.

In his effulgent joy, Peter Morris — for it was he that saved the accused, who was none other than Mr. Mogens — embraced Babette in the court-room. The judge thought this enough for the serenity of a court of justice, and dismissed the case. Babette and her lover left the court-room first, and the former did not see her master.

The latter, however, had made a wonderful discovery while locked up in a cell; for be it known that it was not laudanum that the providential druggist had given Mr. Mogens, but plain every-day brandy. The city physician diagnosed the case at once, and Mr. Mogens was locked up on a charge of misdemeanor. As he was in the cell, Mr. Mogens reviewed his case. His failure at self-destruction, instead of causing him dejection, filled him with mirth. How ludicrous the entire business was,— the exchange of his garments for that green coat, which was much too small for him! Now he also remembered that his pocket-book, which contained valuable papers and checks, was in the coat he had given to that flower-thief, and what did he get in return? Nothing. He put his hand in the breast pocket,— ah, there was a letter addressed to Mr. Peter Morris. Who was he? He did not care. Unconsciously he drew the letter from the envelope and opened it. It made him stagger. The letter began: "My darling Peter." Oh, the mixed feelings of agony and hope! So, after all, it was not Pety Baglow his wife had been writing to, but to this stranger, whom he knew not, but whom chance had thrown in his way. In his excitement, he did not notice that it was not his wife's handwriting at all. He read on; he was perplexed still more; the letter was signed "Babette." Did his wife use her maid's name as a guise? Certainty, — if he could get but certainty. Now he was a prisoner in a filthy cell. He shook the iron bars; he wanted to be free, — to find out if life was worth living after all.

VII.

"Here, driver," cried Mr. Mogens, as soon as he had reached the street from the Old City Hall, — he had the green coat and hat on, — "there is ten dollars for you; race for your life up to Mogens's place." He was in the cab, and, but a few minutes later, at the feet of his wife.

Well, she laughed and wept as she kissed

his dear head. But he took from his pocket that fatal love-letter, and asked her, for the love of heaven, to explain its startling evidence. Mrs. Mogens read the letter, and uttered such a peal of laughter that both Babette and her lover, who were waiting to call on Mrs. Mogens to acquaint her with future plans, rushed into the room.

"O monsieur," cried Babette. "My Petair's coat!"

"And my letter!" cried Mr. Morris.

"I wrote that copy for Babette," said Mrs. Mogens, with a laugh. "And you were jealous, dear hubby; naughty man to go away before the anniversary."

"My darling, I love you more than I can tell," said Mr. Mogens; "and the thought that you might be unhappy with me drove me mad; forgive me."

It was a picture fit for an artist's brush.

There they stood embraced, both the millionaire and his wife, who never knew of her husband's attempted suicide, and the humble servant with her lover. And the cabman below swore that the "bloke" in the green coat was a dead beat.

A MIDNIGHT SONG.

FINALE.

THE night was calm and glorious. Not a breath of wind, nor a cloud in the sky. The moon threw her silver light in one gigantic beam upon the ocean, and the stars glittered in their iridescent background, while our ship, *The Homeless*, gently rocked upon the heaving bosom of the deep. Of the thousand passengers on board nearly all were on deck. Almost every nation of the civilized world was represented. They were steering for the land of freedom and endeavor,—America. They were remarkably quiet at this moment; were they awed by the grandeur of the ocean? Probably.

Suddenly the trumpet-like voice of the Captain broke the silence. Every one started.

"Let us have a song, ladies and gentlemen. Give us a nice song, a song in which all may join."

"O yes, sir; please, sir," chimed an Anglo-Saxon maiden from the county of Yorkshire; "let us have a genuine English song, sir. I propose, sir, we sing, 'God Save the Queen,' sir."

"I beg your pardon," said a portly German; "the Queen is nothing to us. Let us sing something that will remind us of loyalty and bravery, and deeds done. Captain, I propose we sing 'Die Wacht am Rhein.'"

"Au diable with the Wacht am Rhein," cried an excitable Frenchman. "Gentlemen and ladies, I humbly crave your pardon; but I must protest against German

A MIDNIGHT SONG.

songs. The best German product is Limburger cheese. I mean no offense. But liberty was won when every man of France sang the one great song, 'La Marseillaise.' Captain, I propose this very popular song."

"Presto, Signor Capitano," said an Italian. "Ah, there is nothing like Italy's great song, 'Patria, mia Cara.' Captain, we sing the Italian song, 'Patria, mia Cara.'"

At this a girl approached the Captain. She was remarkably beautiful, and as the moonlight fell upon her figure, she looked like one of those forms modeled by the Greek masters, the poise and symmetry of which take the soul captive, and fill the heart with longing.

"Ladies and gentlemen," she said, and her voice sounded soft and melodious, like the deep, melting tones of a flute. "I am an American. My patriotism, though strong, is rather cosmopolitan. But an

American neither fights nor sings for trifles, being ready, however, to do both for the blessings of his home. If I understand the Captain correctly, it is his intention that we should have a song to inspire the soul and fill the heart with memories and hopes. To accomplish this, you must sing a song to voice the sentiments of all on board. But for this you need not go to London, Paris, Berlin, or Rome. The name of the ship we are on is quite suggestive of the general feeling, — 'Homeless'! Are we not homeless just now, floating between life and eternity? And what could possibly be nearer to our hearts, from whatever country we may hail, than the thought of home, and those loved ones we left behind us? I am certain there is no one on this ship who would not fall in with those who sing 'Home, Sweet Home.'"

"Alas, yes! there are," said a man in the

immediate vicinity of the charming and eloquent American. "Yes, miss, there are over two hundred heart-broken Jews below in this ship, who would rather lament as did their ancestors, 'By the waters of Babylon, there did we sit and weep, remembering thee, O Zion!' We had homes and happiness, but the Czar's cruelty and the mob's brutality robbed us of both. Let those sing of a sweet home who have homes, but to us, homeless wanderers of nigh on two thousand years, to us home is a stigma and a curse. It is very hard to be driven from the land of your birth, to be declared homeless, but it is harder still to join in a joyous chorus when one's soul is in agony and the heart is broken."

And the poor man covered his face and wept.

"My friend," said the beautiful American, "you should not weep over past misfortunes. You are going to a land of liberty, and your future happiness will far outweigh your past misery. In suggesting the song, 'Home, Sweet Home,' I thought of you also. I thought of all those that are homeless. While it is true that some of us are returning to old-established and happy homes, still others, and those are by far in the majority, go to America to found homes and rear families. A few years hence and your past life will be like a dream, aye, a bad dream, but gone and forgotten. You and your people will be citizens of a great republic, respected and honored by all. Some of America's best citizen's are of your faith, who, coming like you, poor and homeless, have made for themselves names, homes, and fortunes. And were you to ask the least of them whether they prefer their old to their new homes, I am certain they would be in favor of the latter. Cheer up, then, my friend, and in anticipation of your future happiness, sing with us of the glory and sweetness of home."

"God bless you, miss," said the Jew, while every one on deck cheered the wise and fascinating girl.

Again the voice of the Captain resounded, but there was a slight tremor in his deep tones as he said, "Let us sing 'Home, Sweet Home.'"

He gave the signal, and the air was filled with the chorus of a thousand voices, some singing and some sobbing, "Home, Sweet, Sweet Home!"

The monsters of the deep rose to the surface, the sea heaved, the moon shone in tranquil beauty, the stars blinked approval. It was a beautiful night; it is a memory now.

We call special attention to our next book, a powerful novel, founded on the great SHARON CASE, entitled:

"SERALTHA,"

BY

ABEL M. RAWSON,

Author of "The Junior Partners."

We have also a new and beautiful edition of

BLACK BEETLES IN AMBER,

BY

AMBROSE BIERCE.

Our Coast Address is

WESTERN AUTHORS' PUBLISHING ASSOCIATION,

MURPHY BUILDING,

SAN FRANCISCO, CAL.